A BRIGHSTONE BOOK OF SEASONS

All the proceeds of this book
will support the nominated charities of the
Brighstone Christmas Tree Festival, which are
sufficiently numerous to satisfy everyone.

The Revd. Tim Eady, Rector of Brighstone

A Brighstone Book of Seasons

Readings and Reflections for the Seasons of the Christian Year

Compiled by
TIM EADY

ESME BOOKS
Brighstone – Isle of Wight

Copyright © Tim Eady 2004

First published 2004

Published by Esme Books
The Rectory, Rectory Lane, Brighstone, Newport
Isle of Wight PO30 4QH

ISBN 0 9548726 0 6

Unless otherwise indicated, biblical quotations are
from the New International Version © 1973, 1978, 1984
by the International Bible Society.

Book design and production for the publisher by
Bookprint Creative Services, P.O. Box 827, BN21 3YJ, England.
Printed in Great Britain.

Dedicated to the saints of the parishes
of Brighstone, Brook and Mottistone: those
from the past who have bequeathed such a terrific legacy,
and given me an awe-inspiring example to follow,
and those of the present who have tolerated my
foibles and shortcomings of the past twelve
years with such good grace and humour.

Contents

Preface

Even after twelve years as Rector of the United Benefice of Brighstone and Brook with Mottistone, I sometimes have to pinch myself to be certain that it really is true. There can be no better place than this anywhere in the whole of the UK. This is a parish of breathtaking scenery, from rolling downs to majestic coastline; astonishing history, from dinosaurs to the present day. This is a benefice of amazing vitality and gifted people, as the following pages will demonstrate.

To be Rector here is a humbling experience. It is not just the three Rectors who have later in life been exalted to Episcopal rank, but virtually all of my predecessors have ensured that this little corner of England has played a significant role in local and national life. From the Tower of London to Port Stanley in the remote Falkland Islands, the clergy of Brighstone, Brook and Mottistone have been there.

But the fame of these villages extends beyond its clergy. If you are looking for heroic soldiers, look no further – two VC holders are remembered here, not to mention notable generals and politicians. Garibaldi passed by. If natural history is your interest, there is something for every taste. Dinosaur bones we have in plenty. Our churchyards contain some of the best natural habitat in southern England. Red squirrels are numbered amongst our parishioners. If you want human interest, we have the nautical equivalent of poacher turned gamekeeper in the smugglers who found respectability overnight with the arrival of the

Island's first lifeboats. The Wilberforce connection adds an international dimension to our social concern. In recent years, the village has brought back a silver medal from the Chelsea Flower Show. If your interests are literary, Thomas Ken's hymns remain amongst the most popular ever. J.B. Priestley lived here. There can be few communities that are so well documented with biographies, memoirs, histories, or depicted in works of art.

By any criteria, the coastline of south west Wight is a fascinating place to live.

This book, however, is not about Brighstone, Brook and Mottistone. This book sets out to explain the seasons of the Christian year: their origins, traditions, and meaning. But because it is *A Brighstone Book of Seasons*, it does so with a local flavour. It includes one or two local traditions and celebrations. Most significantly, each season is illustrated with the writing of local authors, past and present. These items are not necessarily intended to describe the particular season, but to offer thoughts, reflections and feelings, which are appropriate to the time of year. Thus, it can be used as a companion to the year, and dipped into as the seasons progress.

Few communities of 2000 souls can boast the wealth of talent, past and present, which exists within these parishes. The one qualification of all the authors quoted in this book is that they live, or have lived at some time in the past, within the parishes of Brighstone, Brook or Mottistone. The great names of our distinguished history mingle with the saints of the present day. My own descriptive sections are based upon talks first produced for local radio, entitled Seasons of the Year. The historical writing is drawn from a variety of sources, primarily the *Brighstone Banner of Faith*, and *Brighstone Newsletter*, but also from other local publications. The writings of the saints on earth have all been contributed voluntarily; much of it has never been previously published. I take on trust that the anonymous poem, *From Lent to Whitsun*, is written by a local person, as it was left for me inside Brighstone Church, and speaks of specific local customs.

My thanks to everyone who has contributed. Special thanks to Chris Goodman, who has studied the text meticulously, made many corrections and suggested numerous improvements.

Revd. Tim Eady,
Thomas Ken Day (8 June) 2004

Notes on the Text

Brisoners This term to describe the residents of Brighstone, is found in the writings of Canon William Heygate in the Brighstone Banner of Faith, and is well remembered by senior local residents.

The Three Bishops Brighstone is unusual to be able to number three bishops amongst its clergy.

Thomas Ken served in Brighstone from 1667–1669, before moving to Winchester. As King's chaplain, he refused to grant house room to Nell Gwyn, going to the lengths of having the roof taken off his Winchester home in order to make it uninhabitable. Despite his fierce opposition to the monarch's immoral life-style, Charles II made him Bishop of Bath and Wells in the last days of his life, a post which Ken held until the accession of William of Orange, when he resigned his bishopric on the grounds that William was not the rightful monarch and he could therefore not take the Oath of Allegiance. Most of his writings in this book date to his time as Bishop, although his hymns were probably written at a much younger age, and could well date to his years in Brighstone.

Samuel Wilberforce was Rector of Brighstone between 1830 and 1840. He was a very young man when he arrived here. His father, William Wilberforce came to visit, and stayed in the Rectory on several occasions before his death in 1833. Samuel went on to have a distinguished career, serving as Bishop of Oxford, and for a short time as Bishop of Winchester before being killed in a riding accident.

George Moberly arrived in Brighstone in 1867, and was Rector for two years. Previously, he had been Head Master of Winchester College. His large family took Brighstone by storm during their short occupancy of the Rectory. Moberly left Brighstone upon his appointment as Bishop of Salisbury, where he served until a very old man.

Dulce Domum An eminently readable biography of George Moberly, written by his daughter, Catherine Moberly.

Charlotte Yonge was a 19th century authoress, and friend of the Moberly family, who paid several visits to the parish during the two years of George Moberly's incumbency. The two oak chairs, which stand in the chancel of Brighstone Church, were her gift to the parish.

General Jack Seely was a distinguished soldier and politician, as well as being a prolific author and great benefactor to the local community. He was created 1st Lord Mottistone in 1933.

The United Benefice of Brighstone, and Brook with Mottistone was formed in 1978. Before this date, there was a Rector in both parishes. The parish of Shorwell was joined to the benefice for a few years in the mid 1980s, hence the reason for the present Newsletter serving Brighstone, Brook, Mottistone and Shorwell. Precisely how long the present distribution of clergy will endure remains to be seen.

Times and Seasons

'To everything there is a season and a time for every activity under heaven.' (Ecclesiastes 3:1)

There is something inevitable about the link between the changing seasons of the year and the development of human society. Each season has its own particular feel, depending upon the weather, length of daylight hours, and in most societies, the continuous cycle of ploughing, sowing and reaping the land.

Twenty-first century western society is unusual, in that for the majority of us, the direct link between the annual cycle of seasons and the basic process of staying alive is not as significant as in earlier centuries.

It is perhaps equally inevitable that the cycle of religious festivals should be influenced by the changing seasons. The pattern of feasts and festivals in the Old Testament is primarily agricultural, with theological significance appended. Agricultural festivals punctuate our own Christian year, although today Harvest Festival is the only one to which we pay any significant attention. The Christian Church has developed its own pattern of festivals, based upon the foundational events of our faith, for the most part following the life of our Lord from birth to His final departure from the earth, but it too uses the changing seasons to provide pictorial language to help us understand their full significance. Hence Christmas falling in midwinter, speaks of the promise of new hope breaking in to the darkness of human existence. Easter, with its message of resurrection, falls on the Jewish feast of First Fruits in the spring of the year when we are surrounded by the evidence of new life. Pentecost, the Jewish harvest festival, is when we celebrate the harvest of the Spirit in our lives.

The Christian year tells a story. Just as the Jewish year tells the story of escape from exile, the giving of the law and foundation of a nation, so too the Church's year tells the story of God's dealings with humanity, through the life, death and resurrection of Jesus Christ. Each season has particular characteristics. There are times of waiting, penitence, sadness and immense joy. In the same way that much of our lives are routine and humdrum, there have to be 'ordinary times' between the festivals, in order for the festivals to stand out as significant.

However, we must remember that ultimately, all seasons are of equal importance, and it is essential that we worship God at every time of year. After all, Australians manage to celebrate Christmas happily in mid-summer, and Easter in the autumn. We are called to live as the people of God every day come rain or come shine. The Christian year, like so many other things, is there to assist us, but not to become a straightjacket. If it gets in the way of worship, then, like anything else, it is time to re-order our priorities, and remember Jesus' teaching that worship should be 'in spirit and in truth' (John 4).

And so, to begin with, we must consider the importance of every day, and then the place of Sunday. Is it the Sabbath? Should we keep it special, as the recent campaign suggested, or is it just another day?

Sufficient Unto the Day . . .

Before we embark upon a book of seasons, we must pause for a moment and remember that every day is unique. Although there may be certain days upon which we can recall specific events, or which have their own particular 'feel', every day is a God-given gift. It follows then that every day is important. Feast days and holy days are important insofar as they direct our attention towards God, and offer us tools by which to understand and live out our faith, but they must never become an end in themselves. All time is sacred, and of equal value, even if there are occasions when we must be involved in different activities. As Jesus reminds his disciples, 'I have come that you may have life, life in all its fullness'. (John 10:10)

A morning hymn

> Awake my soul, and with the sun,
> thy daily stage of duty run;
> shake off dull sloth, and joyful rise
> to pay thy morning sacrifice.
>
> Redeem thy mis-spent time that's past,
> live this day as if 'twere thy last:
> improve thy talent with due care;
> for the great day thyself prepare.

Let all thy converse be sincere,
thy conscience as the noon-day clear;
think how all-seeing God thy ways
and all thy secret thoughts surveys.

By influence of the light divine
let thy own light in good works shine;
reflect all heaven's propitious ways
in ardent love and cheerful praise.

Bishop Thomas Ken

A prayer for the day

LORD, for to-morrow and its needs
I do not pray;
Keep me from any stain of sin
Just for to-day:
Let me both diligently work
And duly pray;
Let me be kind in word and deed
Just for to-day,
Let me be slow to do my will—
Prompt to obey:
Help me to sacrifice myself
Just for to-day.
Let me no wrong or idle word
Unthinking say—
Set thou thy seal upon my lips,
Just for to-day.
So for to-morrow and its needs

I do not pray,
But keep me, guide me, hold me, Lord,
Just for to-day.

Bishop Samuel Wilberforce

It is – is it

It is the light of day I see
Another chance to live.
Is it the start of something new
A chance to be, to give?

It is the night, time of rest
Moon rising way up high.
Is it time to reflect
Why do we live then die?

It is the countryside so green
A joy to have and see.
Is it ours just on loan
Each flower, grass and tree?

It is a mystery to all
This wondrous place we live.
Is it a moment in earth's span
Our little time to give?

It is ourselves who we are
That matter, make a part.
Is it then not right that we
Listen to our heart?

Jessie Booth

From Fear and Be Slain

Those who have read anything of what I have written, either in this book or elsewhere, will have perceived that my philosophy is that every peril has its providence; that in some mysterious way what appears to be a disaster may well prove to be a blessing, and over and over again, things which seem hopeless come right in the end.

General Jack Seely,
The 1st Lord Mottistone

Sunday

'Very early on the first day of the week, just after sunrise, the women came to the tomb.' (Mark 16:2)

The fact that Sunday is our day of rest and worship is so ingrained within us that we can easily forget that for the first Christian believers, who were all good members of the Jewish race, Sunday was just a normal working day: the first day of the week. The Book of Genesis reminds us that it was on the seventh day of the week that God rested. In the Jewish faith, the Sabbath remains the seventh day of the week, which is, of course, Saturday. The first Christian worshippers continued to meet on the Sabbath, and if they met on the first day of the week at all, it would have been in the evening, after work. However, Sunday was the day of Resurrection. This was the day on which Jesus broke bread with the disciples at Emmaus, and so it was natural that the early Christians would want to use this day for the celebration of the Eucharist.

It was the Emperor Constantine who originally decreed that Sunday should be the statutory day of rest across the Empire, and it is often referred to as the Christian Sabbath. But there is a difference. It was in six days that God made the earth. The seventh day is the original day of rest. The first day of the week is a sign of new activity. Just as God began His creative work on the first day of the week, so He begins the work of re-creation on the first day of the week. So Sunday is a reminder of God's creative activity, first of all in creation, and secondly in renewal and resurrection.

The importance of Sunday

And this, brethren, is the way in which I wish we might come to regard our Sundays. They are to be days of holy rest and sacred peace; days on which we are to put away common work and common things; days on which we are to go to Church and turn our leisure to the thoughts of God and Heaven; days as like as we can make them to days of heaven in the midst of the work and weariness and troubles of the world; days which are not to be gloomy or sad days, still less days of riot or intemperance or vicious idleness; but days of kindly tempers, of sober joy, of good Christian reading. . . . Each Sunday as it comes commemorates all the great things that God has done for us.

Bishop George Moberly,
from Parochial Sermons, mainly from Brighstone

Childhood memories

Many of the pews were traditionally allotted to various homes, and the Prior's Cottage pew was just behind the Rectory pew. As a little boy, I used to count the 'Amens' during the service; at Eastertide, I would count the 'Alleluias' instead. I think the score was over thirty. Of course, the sevenfold Amen was a bonus!

Dorothy (my sister), was given lessons on the organ by Miss Scalding, the organist at Shorwell Church. The Brighstone organ was single manual and blown, of course, by hand. The 'blower' watched a little weight attached to a chord, which moved up and down according to the wind pressure, a mark indicating when it was time to start pumping again. I was Dorothy's blower when she was practising. If she was playing a simple exercise, not much wind was necessary, so I used to wander around the church looking in the hymnbooks etc. All of a sudden there would be a horrible wail and I would rush back to my handle, being the target for poor Dorothy's withering looks. When she became more proficient and tackled more difficult pieces, I needed to work quite hard, especially for 'Baal we cry to thee'. Dorothy was soon able to play for the Sunday afternoon children's service.

Rollo Denys Lempriere,
from Brighstone . . . and afterwards

Advent

The Christian year begins, not on New Year's Day, not even with the birth of our Saviour, on Christmas Day, but four Sundays before Christmas, on Advent Sunday.

Advent literally means 'Coming'. It is a serious season, containing many profound themes, but always tinged with the feeling of expectation and hope. We look for the coming of God amongst us. In reality, much of the solemnity of the Advent season is lost in the flurry of activity that precedes Christmas, but these weeks should be a time for waiting and preparation.

We think about the coming of God into our world – God breaking into human history. This is a time for awe and wonder. As we recall the first coming of God, as a baby at Bethlehem, we remember the stories of those who prepared the way for that coming: the prophets of the Old Testament; John the Baptist, who echoes the message of Isaiah the prophet, 'Prepare the way for the Lord!', and Mary, the mother of Jesus, who meekly submitted herself to God's will – 'Behold, I am a handmaid of the Lord, let it be to me according to your will'.

With Mary's example to encourage us, we must also remember that God comes to us today, and invite Him into our hearts and lives, as we seek to live as His people in our own age. Hence this is primarily a season of challenge, as we recall the future coming of our Lord, at the end of time, when all things will be made new. So, the four great themes of

Advent are death, judgement, heaven and hell – not easy subjects for us to think about, but ones which remind us of our mortality, and the transience of human life.

The colour of the season is purple – a royal colour, a solemn colour – as we contemplate the sovereign rule of God over our lives, tempered, on the third Sunday of Advent with pink, a reminder of the joy of our faith, 'Rejoice in the Lord always and again I say rejoice' (Philippians 4:4).

Advent offers us the opportunity to remember that we live with a foot in two time zones simultaneously: now and eternity. Perhaps the most important 'coming' that we should remember is the coming of God into our hearts and lives today every time we open ourselves up to him.

The Advent Call

The season of Advent is with us. It's solemn call is sounding in our ears. It bids us get ready to meet our Lord at His coming. If we are to prepare ourselves, it must be by earnest thought and prayer: by striving to watch with Him at every opportunity.

Revd. Ernest Silver,
Brighstone Banner of Faith, *December 1903*

Waiting

Life is a journey . . . we pause . . . we wait . . .
time to look back – reflect on past memories –
time to turn over the concerns of the present –
time to hold on to the hopes of the future.

We wait.

The young mother feels life stir within her as she
    waits –
sometimes fearful – apprehensive – eager –
    impatient
waiting to hear the first cry of her new born child.

The young child waits –
Will Father Christmas bring that longed for toy?
The teenager waits –
footsteps herald the arrival of the postman
With fearful trembling hands the letter is opened –
revealing those long awaited exam results.

Waiting – hands clenched – head lowered, we wait
Will it hurt? Oh hurry up!
Then the summons to the dentist's chair.

The young girl waits – will he phone?
A surge of impatience – can't wait – tone ringing out!
Please answer – no reply – just have to wait!

Waiting – a restless night – tossing and turning –
the mind churning over all those problems – we lie
    and wait
will sleep ever come?
The dawn breaks – bringing with it
stillness and calm to our troubled minds.

He waits.

As we step out into the world to face a new day
the door is shut – yet He patiently waits outside
silent – still
His journey is over – ours has just begun
If – with eager and expectant minds
we open the door of our hearts and let Him in
Our waiting will be over.

Petrena Camps

December

The shops are bright with tinsel,
Children's faces shine
With such expectation
For it's nearly Christmas time.

Busy people hurry,
No time to stop and stare,
Soon the Christ Child's birthday
Which everyone can share.

Peggy Thompson

Advent during the Boer War

You know, I think, dear brethren, how grieved I have felt
year after year at the poor attendance at the Week-day
Services in Advent and Lent. I know that few can come,
and that it is an effort and a sacrifice to those few. Ah! How
good if it be a sacrifice, how much we need and owe self-
sacrifice! But now this Advent, my dear friends, this
Advent when our fellow countrymen are dying for
England's sake, and when their relations are mourning

bitterly – this Advent I say especially let there be much prayer and constant intercession. It is the least you can do. God give you grace to do it with all your hearts.

Canon William Heygate,
Brighstone Banner of Faith, *December 1899*

Christmas

It may come as a surprise to discover that Christmas did not exist for the first three centuries of the Christian era. The great feast of Easter, with associated events, was celebrated from the very earliest Christian days, but Christmas only became popular as the faith became established and settled in Europe. Today it is the most widely observed Christian festival in the calendar. For many, it is the only Christian festival of which they are properly aware, although many of the trappings that we take for granted date back no further than Victorian times.

At the heart of Christmas lies a mystery – the wonderful reality of God Himself taking human form and being born on earth. We may question how He did it, we must surely meditate upon why He did it, but the stark reality is that He did do it. Such is the reality of the Incarnation – God in human form. This makes Christmas a 'holy night'. The thought of God taking human form is the most awe-inspiring event imaginable.

Of course, we don't know the date of Christ's birth, (late September, round about the Jewish Feast of Tabernacles is one favoured possibility), but December 25th has been used as the occasion to mark the event since early in the 4th century. For the Romans, this date marked the winter solstice, and in the year AD 274, the Emperor Aurelian established it as the festival of the birth of the sun. This pagan festival was adopted as the Christian festival of the birth of the Son of God sometime following the conversion of the Emperor Constantine in AD 312.

So the pagan festival was 'converted' to a Christian festival, possibly as an attempt to eradicate sun worship, and establish Christianity as the dominant religion, but the comparison between worship of the sun – the source of light and warmth, and worship of God – the source of our spiritual light and life, are self-evident.

The great sadness of the Christmas season is that it has never completely shaken off its pagan origins, and there have been various attempts to curb the excesses of revelry – most notably under the rule of Cromwell in the 17th century, when Christmas was outlawed, and feasting was declared illegal. In the increasingly secular culture of present day Britain, Christmas appears again to be reverting to a secular festival, even with over zealous political correctness renaming the feast 'winterval'. So that leaves all the more reason for a re-discovery of the real meaning of the Incarnation.

The colour of the Christmas season is white, or more properly, gold – the colour of major festivals.

God with us – the Clergy speak

God with us – doesn't that make you stop and gasp and then rejoice? No wonder Christmas is a time for laughter, for joy, for singing, for God has come amongst us in the birth of Jesus, His Son. Jesus took on human, tangible form, to enable us better to both understand and relate to Him.

Revd. Paul Wilson, Curate,
Brighstone, Brook and Mottistone Newsletter,
December 1984

If you would spend a happy and a blessed Christmas come to greet your Saviour in the early morning hour, offering to Him the best place in your loving heart.

Canon William Heygate,
Brighstone Banner of Faith, *December 1892*

Christmas recalls to our minds, not merely a time for festivity, but festivity for a reason. The reason is that, 'God so loved the world that He gave His only begotten Son, that all those who believe in Him should not perish, but have everlasting life'. So to us, Christmas is both a memorial and a Thanksgiving. We show our thankfulness by worshipping God on Christmas Day, and by trying to live in and by His Spirit all the days of our life. I hope you will make a special effort to join the family of God in the worship of their Father on Christmas Day and on every Lord's Day.

Revd. Ralph Charlton,
Brighstone Church News Sheet, *December 1962*

A Headteacher remembers . . .

The first Christmas I was here, it was decided to hold a Carol Concert and Nativity Play in the church. The Rector made it quite clear that although he would support the idea, no form of heating could be provided. So various paraffin heaters were loaned by parents to heat the vestry area where the children would dress. Prior to the service, I went to ensure that everything was all right. However, I was met with a smoke filled church. One of the heaters had caught fire. Acting quickly, I carried it out into the church-yard. Now, with the building full of fumes, we had to open

all the doors losing the little bit of heat we had built up. We
hope no one noticed!

John Ball,
Headteacher of Brighstone School 1961–1968

A sonnet for Christmas Eve

Dear God! Grant us to have a Christmas white,
For it is seasonable and so apt,
That snow should fall from heaven for Christmas
   night.
Then starlit silence and a world so rapt
In kind thoughts, and mystic contemplation.
The crunch of our feet in snow, crisp and cold,
Our hands in gloves, losing all sensation,
With gay papered parcels, red, green and gold
Bringing our children's Christmas happiness.
Excitement has given way to slumber,
And tousled heads upon their pillows press
And they'll awake to joyfulness and wonder . . .
But do the homeless also love the snow,
With no roof, no warmth – nowhere else to go?

Robert Courtney Walker

A thought for Christmas Eve

To you who come but once a year,
To sing a hymn or say a prayer,
Please spare a thought for those
Who sweep the floor and dust the pews,
Play the organ, arrange the flowers,
Read the lesson, polish the brass,
And more beside for casual visitors who pass by

To visit and expect of right
To use the Church by day or night,
In life and death: baptism, marriage or funerals,
Though they may not have attended a service
Since last year's Christmas Eve.

Angela Clarke

The shepherd boy's Christmas

Father, may I come with you, to help you watch the
 sheep?
And father, may I take the crook you promised I
 might keep?
I will not be a nuisance; I'll do as I am told,
And wrap up in my warmest cloak to keep me from
 the cold.
Shall I light the fire now to keep the wolves at bay?
I would not like for them to come and take our
 lambs away.

Oh father, can you tell me, why is the sky so bright?
There is a sort of silence, such a light in the dark
 night.
We can see each other clearly, and the sheep look
 snowy white,
Who is that man, my father, standing tall and still?
The light is coming through him, we hear him and
 we thrill,
What is he saying, father, about a new king born
 today?
Born in a stable lowly, and not so far away.
In our town of Bethlehem, how ever can this be?
But he is saying, father, that we must go and see,

We're only humble shepherds, what can we take a
    king?
We have nothing worthy to make Him an offering.

Father, look, he's not alone, there are many more
And they are all singing glory, as I've never heard
    before.
The glorious light is fading now and we must find
    this babe
And tell the other folks around so that they too
    might bow.

I've looked at Him, my father, the baby in the stall,
He doesn't look like royalty, not like a king at all.
But the angel said he's precious, the Son of God on
    high,
and we must spread His message to everyone
    nearby.
He's smiling at me father, and there's a light around
    his head,
I'm sure now that we were led, to visit at this stable,
As this tall angel said.

I've nothing much to leave with Him, oh I know
    what I'll do,
I'll give him the crook you gave me, I'm sure he'll
    love it too.
I have the strangest feeling what the angel said was
    true,
That he will grow to be a king, but be a shepherd
    too.

Peggy Thompson

The light of Christmas

Light a Christmas candle,
And remember as you do
The light sent into the world
At Christmas time for you.
The Lord who gave His only Son
A child in manger stall,
A light to shine in darkness
To lead us when we fall.
If we would stop and wonder
Amid the tinsel and the snow
The babe within that manger
Who came so long ago
Is with us still to help us
He will answer when we call
The light that came at Christmas
Is shining bright for all.

Peggy Thompson

Love came at Christmas

Let there be cards, let there be candles,
But let there be love.
Let there be turkey, and warmth by the fire,
but let there be love.
Let there be snow on a damp Christmas morning,
Let there be crackers, pulled without warning,
Let there be happiness, full in our hearts,
But let there be love in far distant parts.

Let there be a hug, for a child who is crying,
A moment of comfort for one, who is dying,

Let there be a loaf for the hands that are reaching,
Let there be a fire, to warm frozen fingers,
Let there be a shelter, oh how winter lingers!
Let there be a message, for the Master above,
Yes, let there be Christmas . . .

> but let there be love.

Fiona Perks

The gift of love

Love, thou sweet and gentle child,
Born of a mother tired and mild,
Laid in golden cattle straw,
Feeling night's cold clammy claw.
The cattle breath will bring thee balm,
While angels sing a happy psalm.

Love, having nought,
By no man's greed will you be bought,
Only our need or cry of pain,
Will never call on thee in vain.
Sleep now, sweet love, sleep while you can,
For you must grow to be a man.

Then you will show us how to give,
And live as you would have us live.

Paula Woodford

The Twelve Days of Christmas

The problem with Christmas is that the weeks leading up to the festival are so hectic that by Boxing Day, for many of us, it's very nearly over. We forget that Christmas is a twelve-day festival. In fact the twelve days of Christmas are by rights the twelve days after Christmas, thus making the twelfth day January 6th – the Feast of the Epiphany. Traditionally, these are days for special thanksgiving, and within them we mark the lives of some significant saints as well as holy days that serve to remind us of the reality of the Incarnation: St. Stephen, the first Christian martyr; St. John the Apostle, whose writings resonate with the full impact of the Christ's life on earth; the Holy Innocents, who remind us that God was born to redeem a world replete with suffering and sin; Thomas à Becket, perhaps the most famous English martyr; and seven days after Christmas Day, the Naming and Circumcision of Jesus. We cannot appreciate the full significance of the Incarnation without also becoming aware of the world that Jesus came to redeem. These twelve days mirror the season of Advent. During Advent we think about the coming of God to man. Now we are reminded of the reverse – the coming of man to God, eloquently summarised in the words of Christina Rosetti:

What can I give him, poor as I am?
If I were a shepherd, I would bring a lamb;
If I were a wise man, I would do my part;
Yet what I can I give him, give my heart.

Boxing Day has its origins in medieval times, as the day on which the church alms boxes were opened, and the money distributed to the poor of the parish, hence the origin of the phrase, 'Christmas Box'.

The Star

> Look, see the shining star above,
> Brighter than others in the love,
> Travelling quietly over sea and land.
> Seems to take men by the hand,
> Leading them to live the loving life,
> Taking over from the strife.
> Newborn love, promised help to man,
> Shows a little of the greater plan.

Paula Woodford

A Christmas challenge

> What is this mystery sublime?
> That's manifest at Christmas time!
> Each year it seems that for a space
> There's more goodwill in every place.
> Why cannot man forget his greed?
> And look to others in their need.
> Mankind today seems all intent
> To change the world to some extent.
> We fail to recognise the truth,
> That Nature's way has stronger roots.
> The Christmas message points a way,
> To bring contentment, come what may.
> The feeling that each Yuletide brings,

Continued in our daily things;
Could change the course our lives may take;
And in good time would generate
The means for all to live in peace
With every living man and beast.
Then should we see realised at last
The wolf and lamb together fast,
In glad contentment, – as foretold.
Oh! Dare we dream to be so bold
And hope to see that in our time
An age of peace for all mankind,
Can come to pass, – a state sublime.
Beginning now at Christmas time.

Jack Camps

Christmas reflections

Winter's here with it's icy blast,
But thank goodness Christmas is gone at last;
I had a lovely Christmas meal next door,
And watched my first DVD till four.

Mirisa sent me pairs of socks,
And a couple of bars of my favourite chocs;
Nigel left some Cockburn's port,
And a wedge of cheese from dear Roquefort.

I've had dozens of cards with wintry views,
And some had written lines of news;
Each year some more get lost or missed, –
Perhaps I'm crossed off someone's list?

I sailed on Christmas Eve all right,
With not another single craft in sight,
It was cold and grey – so true to form,
But then back home so nice and warm.

I've still got 'Penny', so I'm not alone;
She had some turkey off the bone.
But Christmas passed without a stir,
And again, no-one brought me any myrrh!

Leslie V. Hall

The New Year

A New Year speaks to us of new opportunities, new hopes, and new resolves. Let us put before ourselves the words above for the opening of 1906: and let us apply them to our religion. We do not expect to get good results in any other work in life, unless we put into it our best efforts, our steadfast and most determined purpose. Have we then any right to expect to receive from our religion that which it is meant to bring us without our giving to it our sincerest and whole-hearted effort and purpose? Certain it is that God expects of us the best we can give – not more but not less; and if we will give that, we shall receive from Him far above all our expectations.

Revd. E. W. Silver, Revd. R. L. Morris,
Brighstone Banner of Faith, *January 1906*

Epiphany – January 6th

Memories of Christmas all too quickly fade into the background, and by the Feast of the Epiphany most people are ready to tidy up their houses, remove the jaded tree and get back to normal.

Epiphany means 'manifestation', or 'showing forth'. In Western Europe, it is the day that we remember the story of the Wise Men – the first Gentile visitors to our Lord, to whom He was made known. Through their story, we remember that Jesus has come into the world to be made known to everyone – Jew and Gentile. In the Eastern Orthodox Church, the concept of 'showing forth' is made even more explicit by moving the story forwards to the baptism of Jesus – the event through which God makes known precisely who Jesus is, by declaring aloud, 'This is my Son . . .'

Epiphany is the time for making explicit the truth that is implicit in the Christmas story. God, who has been born a human baby, and lives amongst us, has come to earth in order to show us His true nature. Further, He calls us to faith and obedience. This is a good season to think about how best to share faith, and to make public the declaration of the gospel. During the weeks of Epiphany we read the stories which point us towards God's activity in the world, as well as in the hearts of His people, such as: Christ's baptism, with its message, 'This is my Son, my Beloved, listen to him'; the call of the first disciples; Jesus first miracle at Cana; the proclamation of the Kingdom of God; and Jesus' own proclamation

of the purpose of his ministry in his visit to the synagogue at
Nazareth. The colour of the season is white. We are still in
festive mood.

The visitors

Shadowed deep, blue-grey and cold,
Lanterns gleam with light of gold,
All worlds watch, wait with baited breath,
So still it is, as still as death.

Then a cry, poor babe how you must fear,
To feel the world, your eyes not clear,
The gentle cattle breathing summer's hay,
Shake the spider's web of fragile grey.

Come the wise men of the East,
Here they'll find no greeting feast,
No wine, no gold, but what they bring,
Little enough of anything.

So lies our hope of life divine.
What hope have I, but in this life of thine?

Paula Woodford

A Gentile festival

Every Gentile in all the world (is) freely admitted, invited,
pressed, urged to accept the blessed grace of God in Christ,
and, by faith and baptism, to become an heir in Christ of
His everlasting Kingdom . . . and for, I suppose, not less
than a thousand years, this little village, like other parishes
in our land has lived under the sunshine of that Light, the

morning star which we celebrate in the Festival of Epiphany. It is the Gentiles' feast; it is our feast . . . But are we indeed living as under that sunshine? The light has come, and we are called to be thankful for it. But there is still terrible condemnation for such as will go on loving darkness rather than light, because they are resolved that their deeds shall be evil . . . If we will go on sinning and will not repent, we are really hating the sunshine, hating the brightness of the Christmas rising . . . Let us rather claim our share in that exceeding great joy with which the Wise Men saw the first brightness of that star when they saw it in the East, and recognized it again when it lighted them to the Saviour's cradle at Bethlehem.

Bishop George Moberly,
from Parochial Sermons, mainly from Brighstone

Whose responsibility?

We could all help, more than a little, to spread the real meaning of Epiphany around. "How?" You may ask. By showing our Lord to the world, by making him manifest to others, through what we say and do – through all our activities as his twentieth century disciples. Witness to our Lord is a total effort involving the entire person and all that person's time. The sooner we all understand this, the better, and the sooner will the Church (a name for you and me) become a more effective power for Christ in and around this place.

Revd. Gordon A. Broome,
Brighstone Newsletter, *January 1974*

Church bells

The Church Bells are the voice, or rather one of the voices of the Church. From the tower, as from the pulpit, they ring out their message of gladness or sorrow, of earnest pleading or reproach to the whole parish.

For centuries they have marked the nation's days of joy and of humiliation, and have rung for the gladness of individual members of the Church, or tolled for them, in turn, to their quiet resting place; solacing the sorrows of the mourners, it may be, with a muffled peal.

But above all, for centuries they have preached the Gospel, as they have marked the facts of our Blessed Lord's life. This is the great purpose of bells. They have rung out with joy – at Christmas, proclaiming the Saviour's birth – at Easter, His Resurrection – at Whitsuntide, the advent of His promised gift of the Comforter; and perhaps on Sunday, the weekly festival of the Resurrection, calling the faithful to the worship of their risen Lord.

Then by contrast, in long seasons of penitence they have spoken no more 'open mouthed to Heaven', but tolled or chimed, in unison with man's feelings of penitence for his owns sins and sorrow for his Saviour's sufferings, finally tolling His death and then speaking no more until they proclaim His joyful Resurrection. Surely no sermon could be more striking than the language of the bells.

Revd. W. E. Heygate,
Brighstone Banner of Faith, *June 1892*

The boyhood of Jesus – a meditation on the Holy child Jesus.

Glory be to Thee, O Lord Jesus, Glory be to Thee, who when Thou wert twelve years old, didst go up to Jerusalem with Thy Parents, after the custom of the Feast, to eat the Passover, and to worship Thy Heavenly Father.

O blessed Saviour, give me grace like Thee, to make Religion my first, and chiefest care, and devoutly to observe, all solemn times, and all holy Rites, which relate to Thy worship.

Glory be to Thee, O Lord Jesus, Glory be to Thee, who when Thy Parents returned home, didst stay behind in Jerusalem, and after three days, wast found of them in the Temple, sitting in the midst of the Doctors, both hearing them, and asking them questions.

O blessed Saviour, who in Thy very Childhood, didst triumph over all the vain delights of youth; and wouldst choose no place, but the Temple to reside in, Mortify in me, all inordinate love of sensual pleasure, which may pervert me from my duty; raise in me an awful reverence of Thy House, an early devotion in my Prayers, and a delight in Thy Praises.

O blessed Jesu, who didst choose before all others, the company of the Doctors, and didst both hear them, and ask them Questions; give me grace to abhor all lewd company, and all filthy communication, give me grace to love wise, and sober, and profitable, and religious conversation, and to be diligent, and inquisitive after learning, and whatsoever is good.

Glory be to Thee, O Lord Jesus, Glory be to Thee, who when Thy Father, and Mother had sought Thee, sorrowing, didst reply to them, How is it that ye sought me, wist ye not that I must be about my Fathers business?

O blessed Jesu, who from Thy infancy didst make it Thy whole employment, to do Thy Fathers will, kindle in me a forward zeal for Thy Glory, that I may consecrate my youth to Thy service, and make it the great business of my life, to know and fear, to love and obey, my Heavenly Father.

Glory be to Thee, O Lord Jesus, Glory be to Thee, who didst at last return home with Thy Parents, and wert subject to them! O blessed Jesu, give me grace to honour my Parents, and Governors, and readily to obey all their lawful commands!

O Lord Jesu, bless me with all abilities of mind and body, that may make me daily increase in my Learning; but above all, bless me with Wisdom from above, and give me Thy Holy Spirit to assist, and enlighten me, that as I grow in Age, I may daily grow in Grace, and in the knowledge of Thee, and in favour with God and Man; and every day more and more conformable to Thy Unsinning and Divine example.

Amen, Lord Jesus, Amen.

Bishop Thomas Ken

Lying alone

'Jesus took the children in his arms, put his hands on them and blessed them.' (Mark 10:16)

Lying alone in my bed
Familiar sounds, familiar faces,
The noise of shuffling feet,
Love locked out.

Lying alone in my bed,
Another day of nothing,
Interminable blankness,
Love locked out.

Lying alone in my bed,
No comforting hand,
No laughter or smile,
Love locked out.

Lying alone in my bed,
Another hour, another year,
My life – 'til death,
Love locked out.

Is anyone out there?
Does anyone care?
A person to hold me
And tell me they're there.

Will you be that person?
To take hold of my hand,
To draw back the bed clothes,
And help me to stand.

Sue Young (after visiting a special needs
'closed' home in Yelatma, Russia)

Plough Sunday

The first Sunday after Epiphany is known as Plough Sunday – the first of the four agricultural festivals which punctuate the year. It is a day that we seldom notice, primarily because most of us, even in a rural parish, have lost the immediacy of the link between the food on our table and the sweat of sowing and reaping which goes into the agricultural industry. Yet our faith reminds us of our utter dependence upon God for all that we enjoy, so it is hardly surprising that a predominantly agricultural society should remember its daily toil in its worship.

The Hebrews of the Old Testament developed a cycle of religious celebrations based upon the growing season. By the 19th century four such festivals were regularly introduced into the annual cycle of the English Church: Plough Sunday, Rogation tide, Lammas Day and Harvest Festival. Between them, they remind us of our dependence upon the land, and its food bearing potential. It is right and proper that we should use these occasions as opportunities for prayer and thanksgiving for God's goodness and providence towards us.

Falling in mid-winter, Plough Sunday is the time to celebrate the long hours of preparation that go into tilling and reaping. There can be no fruit and no harvest, without the initial effort of preparation: digging, manuring and preparing the ground. More than that, it is also the time to celebrate the miracle of the growing cycle in which empty fields will blossom into new life yielding a harvest. Plough Sunday reminds us not to take the growing cycle for granted, but to acknowledge our dependence upon God.

In spiritual terms, this is a day that reminds us of the importance of digging over the fallow ground in our hearts. If we are to show evidence of the fruit of the Holy Spirit in our lives, we cannot simply sit back and wait for them to appear. Effort must be put in to achieving the right result. Plough Sunday could equally well be called Prayer Sunday. As we come close to God, we seek His help in preparing our hearts in order that we may cultivate the right kind of seeds in our lives, and so produce a good harvest.

A thought for January

> Crisp and cold is the morning,
> When the day has dawned,
> The white hard frost has covered
> The garden and the lawn.
>
> The earth is hard as iron,
> The trees are stark and white
> Standing in such beauty
> In the morning light.

Peggy Thompson

A white winter

Since Christmas, the whole Island has suffered one of the worst blizzards in its history, and there is warning of worse to come. So far, I have not heard of any casualties, and I hope that there will be none. Such weather, though seasonable, is bad for man and beast alike.

Revd. Ralph Charlton,
Brighstone News Sheet, *January 1965*

Winter begins

A deserted park with empty bench, the trees stand
    stark and bare;
Wind whistling cold among the leaves that litter
    everywhere;
No flowers to see, no buds on bough, all is brown
    and grey,
Everywhere deserted, drab, on this early winter day.
No singing birds, no sun's ray, the people stay at
    home,
Nothing moves except the wind, he's always ready
    to roam,
Winter has begun again, cold, cloudy days in store,
Rain and snow, winds that blow, 'til spring comes
    round once more.

Jessie Booth

Candlemas

Forty days after Christmas we celebrate The Feast of the Presentation of Christ in the Temple, otherwise known as The Purification of St. Mary the Virgin. More commonly, it is known as Candlemas. As a festival it is often overlooked, but rightly stands as the culmination of the Christmas and Epiphany cycle. This is the day on which we recall the last story of the infancy narratives – when Jesus, at forty days old, was taken to the Temple, in accordance with Jewish custom, to be presented to God. St. Luke (Chapter 2), records the event, although a straight reading is a little confusing as there are two strands to it.

The Presentation of Christ is in accordance with the law of Exodus 13: the first-born of every womb should be given to the Lord and redeemed through the sacrifice of a lamb, a reminder of the exodus from Egypt. The Purification of Mary follows the law given in Leviticus 12. Any woman who gave birth was required by law to be purified by taking her offering to the priest for sacrifice. St. Luke infers that Mary brought a pair of doves or two young pigeons, possibly signifying that Christ was born into a poor family – pigeons being an alternative offering for those who could not afford to supply a lamb.

So much for the Jewish background – the significance of the day for Christians lies in the meeting in the Temple between the holy family and two elderly prophets, Simeon and Anna, who immediately recognise Jesus for who He is – God's Son, who will usher in the New Covenant, and offer a permanent means of salvation for all who respond to Him. There is a double edge to this story: joy at the discovery of the coming Messiah, but also the solemn warning of suffering to come which points towards Christ's passion. This pivotal festival takes a final look backwards to Christmas, but also points forward to the reason for Christ's coming – his redemptive work upon the cross. Once this day has passed, we cease to think about Jesus the child, and look towards his adult ministry. In no time at all, Ash Wednesday will be upon us.

Simeon's words are, of course, familiar to all devotees of Evensong as the *Nunc Dimittis*:

> Lord, now lettest thou thy servant depart in peace: according to thy word.
>
> For mine eyes have seen thy salvation, which thou hast prepared before the face of all people;
>
> To be a light to lighten the Gentiles: and to be the glory of thy people Israel.

It is probably from this final verse that the medieval custom of Candlemas arose. It became the day on which candles were blessed for use in church throughout the year, and were distributed to the faithful. We, living in the days of instant electricity, tend to forget the importance of artificial light for societies that were governed by the rising and setting of the sun. Further, light has always been a powerful symbol of the proclamation of the gospel: Christ, the light of the world.

Christ is coming

"Christ is coming, Christ is coming",
Israel sang in deepest woe,
Looking for the Lord to ransom

them from exile, fire and foe.
But their great misunderstanding
saw Christ as an earthly king,
Not the Lamb of God who suffered
Everlasting life to bring.

"Christ is coming, Christ is coming",
as a baby Jesus came.
Simeon of great age awaited
in the Temple for that day.
"Sovereign Lord as you have promised
take your servant now – with joy,
Eyes have seen your great salvation
God has come as human boy."

"Christ is coming, Christ is coming",
Loud "Hosanna" was their cry.
then they mocked him and they scourged Him.
Led Him to the cross to die
but the grave could never hold Him.
Jesus rose as Saviour, King.
Death is vanquished, hell is broken,
"Alleluia", heaven sings.

"Christ is coming, Christ is coming",
down the ages saints have sung,
In the midst of persecution,
and the reign of sin and wrong.
How much more, Lord, do you tarry,
Ere your great triumphal day?
Come Lord, quickly so that we may
share in your eternal sway.

Ivor Debney

Ordinary time: Septuagesima, Sexagesima and Quinquagesima

Depending upon the date of Easter, the period between Candlemas and Ash Wednesday can be anything between three days and five weeks in length, and in the most recent prayer book, Common Worship (2000), is given the bland title of 'Ordinary Time'. The Book of Common Prayer, on the other hand, gives the three Sundays before Lent a much more interesting feel with the splendid titles of Septuagesima, Sexagesima and Quinquagesima. Literally, these Latin words mean seventy, sixty and fifty days before Easter respectively. As we don't have a ten-day week, the titles are clearly meant to be approximate, and have no particular theological meaning. But they are such wonderful words that it would be a tragedy to lose them, and for that reason alone, I like to use them. These weeks are often the coldest and bleakest part of the winter – and remind us that for much of our time, we just have to get on with the daily grind of living.

In ordinary time, the liturgical colour is green – the background colour of God's creation.

A walk by the sea

As I walk upon the virgin sands, untouched by influence or desire of man, my feet leaving scar-like rifts in the filigree crust of gold, all feelings of trespass leave my mind and I am left with only the beach itself, not the sight of it, for that would only clip the wings of its splendour, but the experience of it. For where sea meets shore, tantalizes all senses like a caress from a fair hand, exciting even the shallowest of minds.

It is a morning of mid-winter, and the sun sits enthroned high amongst the clouds, a scream of orange upon the screen of sapphire. Yet the scream is unheard below and only a gentle fade of pale warmth is caught upon my face. The sun's brightness shatters upon the waves, breaking into thousands of tiny shards, silver and pearl, which leap towards my onlooking eyes, but light alone can do little more than reveal a scene of icy serenity.

A gentle breeze blows, herald to bitter winds. Ghostlike, its visage appears, as if mantled by a mist, answering the call of my senses, bowing to bring me offerings of touch, taste, sight, smell and sound. Softly the sea air fills my lungs, hiding from me the keenness of its edge. Mingling scents of salt, sand and the slow decay of beached vegetation comes together to form a brew which enters, thickly, into my body.

All around me stand the warnings of the desolate weather beaten faces of cold rock. Long months have passed since the warmth was stripped from their cores and thrown in tatters to the wind. Yet despite the nagging in the back of my mind, I remain encapsulated and look on.

The ever-growing mixture of despair, memory and anticipation taking hold of me, I continue to walk, drawn on by the sea's siren call, the depth of silence pierced only by the cries of gulls, the soft lapping of the blanket waves in mock imitation of the pulse of my footsteps moving ever onward, in the shadow of the looming cliffs.

Irony, as it seems, is a perfect summer's day spited by winter and left hollowed, an oak bough flayed by lightning. There is no warmth, no sound of children playing; the waves are no longer furtive. My path cuts through all that remains, the pyres of cuttlefish skeletons and dead shells, away from the beach to the far horizon.

Christopher Parsonson

Education Sunday

The third Sunday before Lent – Septuagesima – is often kept as Education Sunday, primarily because the theme for this Sunday in the 1980 Prayer Book, (the Alternative Services Book), was Christ the Teacher. This is a day to pray for schools, teachers, young people, and everyone involved in the world of education. Brighstone has benefited from a Church of England School since 1814. Initially, according to its original Trust Deed, it was established 'for the instruction of children and adults, or children only of the labouring, manufacturing and other poorer classes in the parish of Brighstone or Brixton, and as far as accommodation will permit in the adjacent parish of Mottistone'. Today, its admission's policy is a little wider, and includes the parishes of Brook and Shorwell, and there is no differentiation on the grounds of class distinction. However, this founding document makes an important point. The Gospel has a bias towards the poor. We, who call ourselves Christians, have a responsibility towards those in any kind of need, whether that need be physical or spiritual. Education for all is a natural extension of that responsibility.

A prayer for our school

> Dear Lord God,
> We thank you for all who belong to the community
>   of our school,
> children, staff, parents, governors and friends.

Help us to learn and to grow,
that we may become the people who You want us to
 be;
through Jesus Christ our Lord. Amen.

Revd. Tim Eady

Examination report for Hulverstone School in religious knowledge in 1907

The Head-mistress and her assistants are to be congratu-lated on the religious work of the school. Throughout, there are evident signs of thorough, honest and good work, such as must be of great value to the children's lives. A full syllabus has been admirably taught in all the classes; very helpful private prayers are well known; the written work and the reputation are both highly creditable.

The children have been trained to enter heartily into the spirit of their religious lessons, and, when they leave, must carry with them a valuable equipment of religious knowl-edge with which to face the battle of life.

Revd. Ernest W. Silver,
Hon. Diocesan Inspector

Childhood memories

Before Christmas there would be a special visit from the school governors or committee. After singing some carols, the chairman would hand out an orange to all pupils, and some other little gift. The village policeman, Mr. Harris, was there, and the Rector presided.

Round about 1914 a Mr. Joad, school inspector, came to check the classes at Brighstone. He questioned the class I was in and I was able to answer several correctly. Afterwards, he said to my father, 'Who was that bright boy?', and father was able to answer, 'My son'. I should add that competition was not very great, although there were some quite intelligent pupils.

Rollo Denys Lempriere,
from Brighstone . . . and afterwards

From life and events in the village school

The film "Saxons versus Vikings" was made. Children acted various scenes on Brook Beach . . . the invasion by the Vikings, the killing of a priest. Alfred burnt the cakes on the school field! A pitched battle took place on Brighstone Downs with a number of girls wearing helmets and beards as there was a shortage of boys. Sound effects were added later in the classroom using saucepan lids.

Dennis Courtney, Head teacher 1969-82,
from A History of Brighstone's Schools

Shrove Tuesday

Traditionally, Shrovetide is three days long – the three days before the beginning of Lent. The word 'shrove' is the past participle of 'shrive', an Old English verb meaning, 'to hear your confession'. So Shrove Tuesday is a day on which to confess your sins to God, and thus prepare yourself for the holy season of Lent.

However, since medieval times, this element of confession has been tempered by a little merriment – the last chance to let off steam and have fun before the devout and solemn season of Lent. It was a chance to eat up all the excess rich food in the house. Pancakes symbolise this for us. In the Middle Ages, tradition and necessity often went hand in hand. The harvest season was long past, and food was at its scarcest during the period of planting and sowing, when the growing season was about to begin a new cycle.

In some places a Shriving Service is still held, most famously at Olney in Buckinghamshire, where a Pancake Race precedes it. The origins of this race are obscure, but tradition says that it dates to 1445, when a harassed housewife, on hearing the church bell ringing for the service, ran to church as fast as she could. Unfortunately, in her haste, she forgot to put down her frying pan, and arrived at church breathless, clutching her pan, complete with pancake, still in her hand! The townsfolk found this so hilarious that they have continued to retrace her mad dash every year since then.

The Idler

There is a man who sits and dreams all day,
Who seeks a haven by the primrose way:
He wanders through golden lands of avarice
To where he hopes to find eternal bliss.
But then, alas . . .

Richard J. Hutchings

Prayer for the faithless

Dear Lord would I humbly pray
And in confessing sins this day
Seek forgiveness in thine eyes
That from repentance good may rise.

Would that I could all men love.
Hate and malice quick disprove,
And in loving, love instil,
The joy which is thy sacred will.

Would my lips and thoughts were pure,
Pure as thine which saints adore.
Would my speech Thy wisdom bless,
So dispelling faithlessness.

Breathe in me, O Lord, Thy balm,
Peace, tranquillity and calm;
Guide my winged imaginings
To reach for Thee in earthly things.

Light Thy flame in this cold heart,
Comfort, courage there impart;
True humility inspire.
Be Christ's example my desire.

Love, humility and faith,
Would they all were mine in truth;
Would for ever from this clay
All sin and anguish pass away.

Richard J. Hutchings

Ash Wednesday and Lent

Ash Wednesday is the first day of Lent. Today, we begin our long period of preparation for Easter. The forty days of Lent have their origin way back in the days of the early church. They remind us of the forty days that Jesus spent in the wilderness before commencing his ministry. They also remind us of the last phase of Christ's life on earth, when he 'set his face towards Jerusalem', and made his final journey southwards from Galilee. But if you count through your diary, you may wonder why there are forty-seven days between Ash Wednesday and Easter Sunday. The answer is simple – Sundays don't count. They are celebrated as feast days, so offer a day off from Lenten austerity.

If you take Ash Wednesday seriously, it is a day for receiving the sign of the cross, in ash, on your forehead, as a sign of repentance and sorrow for your sins. The custom derives from a very ancient tradition, when ash was sprinkled over the heads of the penitents, with the solemn warning, 'Remember that you are dust and to dust you shall return; turn away from your sin and be faithful to Christ'. The Collect for Ash Wednesday is the ultimate penitential prayer. We say, 'Create in us new and contrite hearts', which sets the tone for the Lenten period.

Originally, Lent was a period of preparation. In the first three Christian centuries, it was a time for instruction and teaching of new converts before their baptism at dawn on Easter Sunday. Only in the Middle Ages did it become a time for self-denial – for fasting and abstinence. People still talk about giving something up for Lent, although this should not be an end in itself but a means of self-discipline, in order to bring us closer to God.

The ultimate goal of Lent is to prepare ourselves for the celebration of the Resurrection on Easter Sunday. The magnitude of this event merits extra time to prepare, in order that we may be ready to celebrate the great feast. So Lent is a good time to think and pray, read a devotional book, and seek to grow closer to God.

The colour of Lent is purple, emphasising the solemnity of this period.

A Victorian Lent

The solemn season of Lent is close upon us. The year is full of God's calls to us in one way or another, and this is one of His most solemn calls – a warning to consider our ways. We need these special calls, for though we hear God's word read, and hear preaching all the year round, it is still as it was when St. Paul preached at Rome, 'Some believed the things that were spoken and some believed not'. At least, it is true that some realise the things which they hear and many do not. But then, it is just this realising which is everything. Pray God that this holy season may enable you truly to know and forsake your sins, serving God better in the future. Do not neglect this gracious call lest it should rise up against you in the judgment.

Canon William Heygate,
Brighstone Banner of Faith, *February 1889*

A Bishop's Lenten message to his clergy

Reverend Brother,

The time of Lent is now approaching, which has been anciently and very Christianly set apart, for penitential humiliation of Soul and Body, for Fasting, Weeping and Praying, all which you know are very frequently inculcated in Holy Scripture, as the most effectual means we can use to avert those Judgments our sins have deserved; I thought it most agreeable to that Character which, unworthy as I am, I sustain, to call you and all my Brethren of the Clergy to mourning; to mourning for your own sins, and to mourning for the sins of the Nation . . .

Remember that to keep such a Fast as God has chosen, it is not enough for you to afflict your own soul, but you must also according to your ability, deal your bread to the Hungry: and rather, because we have not only usual objects of Charity to relieve, but many poor Protestant Strangers are now fled hither for Sanctuary, whom as Brethren, as members of Christ, we should take in and cherish.

That you may perform the office of public Intercessor the more assiduously, I beg of you to say daily in your closet, or in your family, or rather in both, the 51st Psalm, and the other Prayers which follow it in the Commination. I could wish also that you would frequently read and meditate on the Lamentations of Jeremiah . . .

But your greatest zeal must be spent for the Public Prayers, in the constant devout use of which, the Public Safety both of Church and State is highly concerned: be sure then to offer up to God every day the Morning and Evening Prayer; offer it up in your Family at least, or rather offer it up in Church, especially if you live in a great Town, and say over the Litany every Morning during the whole Lent. This I might enjoin you to do, on your Canonical Obedience, but for Love's sake I rather beseech you . . .

Be not discouraged if but few come to the Solemn Assemblies, but go to the House of Prayer, where God is well known for a sure Refuge: Go, though you go alone, or but with one besides your self; and there as you are God's Remembrancer, keep not silence, and give Him no rest, till He establish, till He make Jerusalem a praise in the earth.

I exhort you to endeavour all you can, to reconcile differences, to reduce those that go astray, to promote universal charity towards all that dissent from you, and to put on as the Elect of God, holy and beloved, bowels of mercies, kindness, humbleness of mind, meekness, long-suffering, forbearing one another and forgiving one another, even as Christ forgave you.

To mourn for National Guilt, in which all share, is a duty incumbent upon all, but especially on Priests, who are particularly commanded to weep and to say, "Spare Thy people, O Lord, and give not Thine Heritage to reproach, that God may repent of the evil, and become jealous for His Land, and pity His people."

Be assured that none are more tenderly regarded by God than such Mourners as these; there is a mark set by Him on all that sigh and cry for the abominations of the Land, the destroying Angel is forbidden to hurt any of them, they are all God's peculiar care, and shall all have either present deliverance, or such supports and consolations, as shall abundantly endear their calamity.

Now the God of all Grace, who hath called you unto His eternal Glory by Christ Jesus, make you perfect, stablish, strengthen, settle you in the true Catholic and Apostolic Faith professed in the Church of England, and enable you to adorn that Apostolic Faith with an Apostolic example and zeal, and give all our whole Church that timely repentance, those broken and contrite hearts, that both Priests and People may all plentifully sow in tears, and in God's good time may all plentifully reap in joy.

From the Palace in Wells,

Feb. 17. 1687.   Your affectionate Friend and Brother,

Bishop Thomas Ken

Spring Clean

Soon 'Spring Cleaning' will be underway in most of our homes. Few would say that it is unnecessary and out of date. The word Lent means Spring. A 'Spring Clean' of the self . . . Do try to use Lent to spring clean your heart and to deepen your love of Jesus.

Revd. Ralph Charlton,
Brighstone Church News Sheet, *February 1964*

Lenten Challenge

This season of Lent is the time when the sap quickens, a time for spiritual refreshment, a time for renewal and strengthening of our faith. Let us not allow this season of opportunity to pass by unheeded; let us all determine that by Good Friday we shall be renewed and strengthened as Christians, a little more worthy of our Lord who gave himself for us on that day.

Revd. Gordon Broom,
Brighstone Newsletter, *March 1973*

Spring

Spring is almost here again
The signs are sure and clear,
Buds bursting on the bough;
Yes, spring is almost here!
Have you seen the snowdrops?
Daffodils will soon appear,
See them bursting through the earth,
Yes, spring is almost here!
Do your days seem longer?
Nights shorter – give a cheer.
Time to stop being a dormouse,
For spring is almost here!
The birds are in full chorus,
They know the time of year,
So give a song to celebrate
That spring is almost here!
Take a look around you,
It's really very near,
The gift of re-creation,
Yes, spring is almost here!

Jessie Booth

First flower of Spring

First flower that thrusts through thawing earth
Contains more joy, more hope, intrinsic worth
Than all the imitative arts of man;
And yet by him how often grows unseen.
Unthinking, beauteous, self-regenerating flower
Irresistible the upward driving power
To search for light! But why?

To live a span of life
That seems to man ridiculously brief?
No time is not important, but the one essential fact
Is continuity of Nature's re-creative act,
Miraculously expressing in colour and perfume,
Eternity enveloped in a single, fragile bloom!

Richard J. Hutchings

Lifeboat Sunday

In a book of Brighstone seasons, it is permissible to include one or two local customs, of which Life-boat Sunday is paramount. The lifeboats of Brighstone and Brook were the first to be established on the Isle of Wight, following a night of horrific loss of life late in 1859. The Rectors of Brighstone and Brook joined forces to launch an appeal, and the boats were soon in service. They continued until modern developments made them redundant, the Brighstone boat last seeing service in 1914, and the one at Brook in 1937. The advent of motor-boats meant that the rowing boats of Brighstone Bay were no longer required, as the coast could be served by the lifeboat at Yarmouth. Lifeboat Sunday in Brighstone and Brook is held in early March, to commemorate the famous rescue on 9th March, 1888, of the SV Sirenia, during which two Brighstone men, one Brook man, and an American sailor lost their lives.

Appeal

It is a matter of painful notoriety, that 14 lives were lost by shipwreck at the back of the Island, about three weeks ago. It was stated by the officers of coastguard and by others at the Inquest, that if a life-boat had been at hand, the whole of these lives might have been saved.

The Revd Edward McAll and the Revd. John Pellow Gaze,
appeal letter 24th December 1859

The Sirenia – March 1888

Let us thank God that our brave fellows have not failed in the hour of danger, but accomplished a gallant rescue from the wreck of the Sirenia, in the terrible sea that was breaking over Atherfield Ledge. Women, children, crew – 30 lives saved, but at how terrible a cost. The loss of our Coxswain and 2nd Coxswain, who were both in the first lifeboat stationed here 28 years ago, and have been instrumental in saving many lives – men who seemed to be as much needed by their families as they were precious to them. But our Heavenly Father knows better than we do, and He has seen fit to order it thus. Let us not doubt either His wisdom or His love.

May their example live long in the parish, and prompt many to a like deed of self-devotion in time to come, if God should see fit to send any in distress to our treacherous shores.

The day on which the Coxswains and the stranger who had died with them were buried, and the deep touching sympathy shown, not only by the whole parish, but by many outside it, for the mourners, are to be remembered for ever in the annals of Brighstone. Probably none of us will ever attend such another funeral.

Our gratitude is due to the Life-boat Institution for its kindly concern in our calamity . . .

Already our boat is in perfect order again, ready for any emergency, and no greater honour can be done to the memory of Moses Munt and Thomas Cotton, than to keep her always so, and well manned.

Canon William Heygate,
Brighstone Banner of Faith, *April 1888*

Launching the boat

In an emergency, the coastguards would inform the lifeboat secretary (who was the local parson) that the boat was needed. Two red rockets would be fired from a gun which made a terrific noise . . .

The life boat and base crew would bring the horses. . . . A minimum of 25 helpers was required. A 'Slipper' was responsible for the chains which secured the boat to the carriage, six horses would be coupled but sometimes the journey commenced with only four horses whilst others were arriving and being harnessed . . .

The carriage had no brakes; helpers would hold the boat back with ropes on the steep access lane to the beach. The crew would be putting on oilskins, sou'westers and boots, and collecting equipment from the lifeboat station.

Once on the beach, the horses would be turned so that the bow pointed towards the sea. The crew would clamber onto the boat the best way they could. A separate line was secured to prevent oars being lost. The chain at the stern and four of the horses were then removed; the two remaining horses and the helpers would push the carriage and boat into the water. Problems were caused by the carriage wheels sinking in the soft sand.

The Bowman would shout launch when a suitable wave arrived, the slipper would release the chain at the bow, helpers would pull on the rope and the rowers would try to get the boat clear . . .

A good time, from the firing of the rockets to launching the lifeboat, was three quarters of an hour.

Robert Cassell,
from Brooke Life Boat *(1997)*

A prayer for travellers

Lord be Thou a guide to the traveller, safety to those that are at sea, a refuge to the oppressed. Be Thou a father to the fatherless, take care of widows, pity and relieve all poor prisoners of debt, and Have mercy on all idiots and mad persons.

Bishop Thomas Ken

Weather or not

There are gales up there in VIKING
But with skies becoming clearer.
More to Norwegian seamen's liking,
Sailing NORTH and SOUTH UTSIRE

With strong winds in the FORTIES,
And with CROMARTY holding FORTH,
TYNE and DOGGER making sorties
Up in FISHER east of north.

There's a deep low west of Denmark,
And a trough in GERMAN BIGHT;
Seas round HUMBER, THAMES and DOVER,
Staying rough 'till west of WIGHT.

Through PORTLAND, west to PLYMOUTH,
And south to BISCAY Bay.
Atmospheric pressure's falling.
And storms are on the way.

FITZROY, SOLE and LUNDY
Have isobars tightly packed:
The FASTNET Race is cancelled
'Till the south west gales have backed.

The IRISH SEA and SHANNON
Wash Ireland east and west,
While ROCKALL's there with MALIN
Surrounding all the rest.

HEBRIDES and BAILEY
Have Scotland in their grips.
While FAIR ISLE, FAEROES and S.E. ICELAND
Punish fishermen and ships.

Ships from all the nations,
Sailing round our shores.
Heed calls from Coastal Stations
To aid their seaward course.

Passing round the top of Scotland
On a course in from the west,
There's TIREE, STORNAWAY and LERWICK,
On the east coast there's FIFE NESS.

BRIDLINGTON calls from Yorkshire:
SANDETTE'S on the sea.
As in GREENWICH AUTOMATIC
And in the Channel Isle, Jersey.

The English CHANNEL proper,
Has it's own Light-Vessel there;
While the SCILLIES and VALENCIA
Help to make the passage fair.

RONALDSWAY's the Manx way,
With many a tale to shed;
Then across the sea to Ireland,
And up to MALIN HEAD.

Then for all the small boat sailors,
How could they ask for more?
Starting clockwise from CAPE WRATH,
All our waters, just inshore.

DUNCANSBY HEAD, including ORKNEY,
Also SHETLAND northernmost,
Then down to Cook's home WHITBY,
Pride of Cleveland's North Yorks coast.

Now down to Kent's NORTH FORELAND
To ST. CATHERINE'S POINT on Wight,
Along the Channel coast of England
To LAND'S END 'ere turning right.

It's passed the Bristol Channel,
And South Wales on the way,
Skirting Anglesey and Bangor
To North Wales and COLWYN BAY.

LOUGH FOYLE in Northern Ireland,
CARLINGFORD LOUGH there to inspire,
Then that westward tip of Scotland,
The lovely MULL OF KINTYRE.

Now CAPE WRATH completes the compass
From Land's End to John O' Groats;
It's a blessing to all those sailors
Who go down to the sea in boats.

Leslie V. Hall

Mothering Sunday

The Sundays of Lent are classed officially as feast days, thus offering an opportunity to break from penitential rigours, but the middle Sunday of the season is especially important. Mothering Sunday, (or Refreshment Sunday as it may also be known) has its origins in medieval times. It was a day upon which priests and people were required by church law to pay a visit to their Mother Church – the original or founding church in the district, normally the monastic centre. This is a day for offering our allegiance to those in whom our spiritual welfare has been vested. The Refreshment title derives from the traditional set gospel reading for the day – the feeding of the 5000.

As early as 1644 there are accounts of this day being used as an occasion for families to meet together. A certain Richard Symonds described it as a 'great day' when children and godchildren feasted with the head of the household. In the 18th and 19th centuries it became the custom for young girls in service to be given the day off, to go and visit their mothers with a gift of spring flowers, or a cake – a Simnel cake. Hence the alternative title for this day – Simnel Sunday. These cakes are rich fruit cakes, disguised on the outside as plain cakes so as not to appear to break the Lenten fast. A traditional Simnel cake is bedecked with eleven marzipan ball, to represent the disciples, but omitting Judas Iscariot.

So Mothering Sunday, which began as a day of homage to Mother Church, has developed into a day on which to lavish gifts upon our mothers. But Mothering Sunday should have a distinctly different emphasis from Mother's Day – an American invention that falls in early May. Mothering Sunday is a day to remember all those who care for and 'mother' us in the course of our lives, and especially those entrusted with our spiritual welfare. We thank God for all that they do for us, and are reminded never to take our carers for granted.

A prayer to be said by children

O my God, give me grace, for the sake of your love,
to honour my father and mother, to render them all
   my love,
reverence and thankfulness,
and all that regard which is due from a child,
that I may pay obedience to their commands,
attention to their instructions, and care for their
   needs,
and may daily pray for their welfare. Amen.

Bishop Thomas Ken

A prayer to be said by parents

O my God, give me grace to imitate your fatherly
   goodness,
and for the sake of your love, to love and to cherish,
   and provide for
to educate, to instruct, and pray for my children,
to take care to give them helpful correction,
and good example, and to make them your children,
that they may truly love you. Amen.

Bishop Thomas Ken

My mother

We were a large family – poor, which was how things were
in the 1930s, but we didn't feel poor because of all the
things Mum would do for us: she made our overcoats,
skirts, summer dresses and her darnings were works of art.
We never wore shoes with holes in the toes – her father had
taught her to sole boots and shoes so that our walking to
school footwear was always sound. Everything was
'serviceable' – a favourite word of Mother's. There were
best clothes for Sunday, worn to Sunday School and Evensong. We were never hungry. . . . It all sounds too good to
be true, I know, but that was the way things were. . . . If all
this care year after year doesn't spell love, I don't know
what does.

Dorothy Cotton remembers her mother

Passiontide

Passiontide encourages us to think about the coming season of the cross. As Lent moves towards its climax, we consider, first of all, the meaning of the cross, before we mark the significant events of the last week of Christ's life on earth. Passion Sunday, the fifth Sunday of Lent, stands as a day to begin the process of considering our Lord's suffering, and to think theologically about the cross – what it meant for Christ then, what it still means for us today. It points us towards the climactic events of Good Friday.

As so often happens, there is an alternative title for Passion Sunday – Care, or Carling Sunday. In Old English, 'care' literally means 'serious concern', or 'suffering', which leads us back to the theme of contemplation upon Christ's suffering. Carlings, in northern England, are dried, grey peas, which are fried in butter, possibly as a way of remembering the austere theme for the day, but also marking the ultimate in Lenten austerity, at a time of year when fresh vegetables were simply not available.

A thought

In Passiontide, it is as if our Lord and Saviour drew very near to us, and bade us come and be with Him in the bitter agony which he bore for us.

Revd. Ernest Silver,
Brighstone Banner of Faith, *April 1905*

The meaning of the Cross

On the cross Jesus demonstrates God's love freely shown. He died in order that humankind may be re-united with God. The next two weeks challenge us to consider the meaning of the cross. We can't properly celebrate Easter, or contemplate the full wonder of the resurrection and promise of new life, without coming first to the cross. Take time, between now and Easter Sunday, to consider the sheer enormity of God's love for you. Then, when Easter Sunday dawns, we can rejoice with a new confidence, as we share in the wonder of God's love for us.

Revd. Tim Eady

Palm Sunday and Holy Week

There's something joyful about Palm Sunday. It's the day when Jesus entered Jerusalem riding on a donkey whilst the crowds waved their palm leaves, shouting 'Hosanna', (Save us Lord). It's the final celebration before the dark clouds of suffering and death intervene. Palm crosses serve as a reminder of how this week will end. The donkey, like much in the story of Jesus, is symbolic. It signified peace. Jesus the King entered Jerusalem, not as a mighty warrior, but in peace.

Since earliest Christian times Palm Sunday has been kept in special ways. As early as the 4th century there was a Palm Procession from the Mount of Olives into Jerusalem. The idea soon spread to Spain and France, and the first recorded procession in England occurred in AD 709. It is an occasion to welcome Jesus into our community, with the reminder that we still live in a world that is crying out for salvation. Every generation must discover its need for Christ for itself.

Palm Sunday leads us into Holy Week, bringing us to the central events of the Christian story. It is impossible to celebrate Easter with full vigour and understanding without first living through the events of Christ's passion. Holy Week confronts us with the reality of Christ's appearance on earth, and rightly holds a critical position in the church's year.

Holy Week contains many well known stories: Jesus overturning the money changer's tables in the Temple; his parables about the end times; the story of the Last Supper; his long discourse with the disciple; and, of course, his arrest, trial and execution. It's a story with tremendous dramatic appeal and larger than life characters: Peter, the man who vows never to desert Jesus and promptly denies him three times; Judas, who betrays the man he has served for three years; Pontius Pilate, who washes his hands of the affair; the anguish of Mary, Christ's mother. There is political intrigue, religious ferment, human psychology – all elements for good drama.

At the heart of Holy Week lies the greatest challenge that any of us can ever face. The book of Hebrews reminds us that 'Christ offered one sacrifice for sin', in order that all who believe in him can approach the throne of God Himself with hearts which have been made clean. God calls for no less than total faith in His Son.

The colour for Palm Sunday is red, symbolic of Christ's blood, shed for the sins of the world.

A solemn week

This is the most solemn week in the year. It is the week of our Saviour's suffering and death. Except for what took place this week we should have no hope of salvation. Except as we, by faith, quickened by love, realise what happened, and apply it to our own hearts so that we are in will and affection, crucified with Christ, we have no hope of salvation. A right use of this week is to help us to realise what is of such importance to us. Try and avoid the world and pleasure. Try and think much of your Saviour's sufferings for you; especially in the quietness of His House, in His immediate presence if you can, and above all on Good Friday. This we say to men, women and children alike, for all have the same need for a firmer faith, and all, as they see the Saviour hanging on the Cross, have the same call to a more unselfish love.

Canon William Heygate,
Brighstone Banner of Faith, *April 1890*

Maundy Thurday

The great climax of Holy Week begins with our Lord's celebration of the Last Supper, which St. Paul introduces by saying,
'On the night before he died'. We tend to lose something of
the sense of continuity between the Last Supper and the
Crucifixion because we have a night's sleep between Maundy
Thursday and Good Friday. For Jesus, however, there was no
night's sleep. The train of action which followed from his last
meal led directly to Gethsemane, his betrayal and arrest, the
desertion of the disciples, trial by night before the Sanhedrin,
his handing over to the Romans, his passion and death. There
is no more appropriate night of the year than this on which to
'watch and pray' as commanded by our Lord.

It is no coincidence that the Last Supper occurred at the
season of Passover. This is the festival at which the Jews
remember how the Lord delivered them from slavery in Egypt
by commanding them to mark their doorposts with the blood
of a lamb, in order that the angel of death should 'pass over'
their homes. Christ himself used this imagery to explain his
own death. John the Baptist describes him as 'The Lamb of
God who takes away the sins of the world', prompting St. Paul
to write, 'Christ our Passover has been sacrificed for us, so let
us celebrate the feast'. Hence the Last Supper has become the
event by which we remember the sacrifice of Christ, taking
bread and wine as He commanded, and sharing them, 'in
remembrance of me'. We continue to share these tokens of
His body and blood, as a foretaste of ultimate glory.

So the Last Supper and Good Friday are not separate events, but are better thought of as the same event: one leads directly to the other. The first provides the background which helps us understand the meaning of Christ's death, the second is the most solemn day in the Christian calendar, upon which we recall the event without which there would be no forgiveness, no salvation, no hope for the future.

The title 'Maundy' comes from our Lord's teaching at the Last Supper, as described in St. John's Gospel, Chapter 13. It is derived from the Latin word, *Mandatum*, which means commandment. Before He washes His disciple's feet, He says, 'A new commandment I give to you, that you love one another, as I have loved you.' From the earliest Christian centuries, it became a custom amongst priests to wash the feet of twelve poor men on this day. Gradually the giving of money, food and clothes was added to this rite. (It was reported this year that the Bishop of Peterborough spent Maundy Thursday afternoon polishing the shoes of passers by in Peterborough High Street.) James II was the last English king to perform this foot washing ceremony, but from then onwards, the ceremony of the giving of Maundy Money by the Sovereign to elderly subjects has never ceased. Our present Queen, Elizabeth II, has been responsible for the movement of this ceremony away from Westminster Abbey to a different cathedral each year. In 1998, local Brook resident Bob Cassell, was a recipient of Maundy Money in Portsmouth Cathedral.

The meaning of the Eucharist

Look at it again thus: 'Whoso eateth my flesh and drinketh my blood hath eternal life, and I will raise him up at the last day'. Do you really know and consider this? It is the very source and support of spiritual strength and life in our own separate souls. The Flesh of Christ here spiritually eaten is meat indeed, and his Blood here spiritually drunk is drink indeed: real meat, real drink, meat and drink to our souls – meat and drink that will feed our souls with Divine life and strength.

Can you do without it? Can you hope to be good, can you hope to please God without it? Would not your bodies die without their proper food? Do you think your souls can live without their proper food? Are you then satisfied with yourselves? Can you be?

Bishop George Moberly,
from Parochial Sermons, mainly from Brighstone

Involved people

The Eucharistic Prayer is a reminder of Christ's sacrifice for us, and a reminder of how we should respond. For it to be meaningful, we must be really involved, not people sitting on the sidelines, but people making the prayer our own, people who are bringing to the forefront of our minds everything that Jesus did for us. This prayer is not for the priest only, just because most of the words are for the priest to say. That doesn't mean that we should switch off until it's our turn to say our bit. . . . We need to be part of it. . . . Our participation should mean more than just words. It should be an experience for all of us. It should bring us to the full awareness of God, a closeness to God that we want to take with us into our everyday lives.

Jean Wavell, Licensed Reader

Good Friday

Hot Cross Buns are the traditional characteristic food for Good Friday. They remind us that this day is significant. It is, of course, the most solemn day of the year, upon which we follow our Lord up the hill of Calvary. 'Good' may appear to be a strange title to give to this day, but in effect it means 'holy'. The 'good' which is derived from this day is the gift of salvation, offered to us through faith in the atoning death of Christ. This holy day offers the opportunity to recall the true meaning of why Christ came to earth, 'to give his life as a ransom for many'.

Through Christ's death:

- we are redeemed – set free from slavery to our earthly nature, and given the liberty of becoming the sons of God.
- we are justified – God has taken our place in the criminal court, and paid our sentence Himself, in order that we may life a new life, set free from the consequences of sin.
- we are reconciled to God, called to be His friends, at peace with Him.

All this, God has done by dying on the cross. Good Friday is His megaphone call to the world, calling us to respond to Him, to receive His love, believe in Him, and commit ourselves to live for Him. There is no better day than Good Friday to renew our commitment to Christ. It is a day for prayer:

Lord Jesus, you went through so much for me. Come and live in my heart, and make me the person who you want me to be. Amen.

The loss of Good Friday as a day for quiet contemplation is to be deplored. On the day of Princess Diana's funeral, in September 1997, when the shops closed and Brighstone Main Road was deserted, one parishioner remarked, 'How come it isn't like this on Good Friday?'. It seems strange that we can accord such respect to a princess, but not for the King of all kings.

All colour is removed from the church for Good Friday. The altar is traditionally stripped bare after Maundy Thursday services, and remains bare until Easter morning.

But Good Friday tells only half of the tale. We must move on to Easter Sunday to discover the culmination of the story.

How to spend Good Friday

Every hour of this solemn day is hallowed by some circumstance of our Lord's Passion, which only ended in His death. And all he suffered was for us and for our salvation. Is it more strange or more sad, that any man who calls himself a Christian should make a holiday of this day, and devote it to pleasure and amusement? And yet, this is the very way in which too many so-called Christians observe it. We earnestly desire the inhabitants of this parish to observe this great day very differently. If it is to be a good Friday and not a bad one to us, it must be spent in sorrowful confession of our sins, and in loving worship of our crucified Lord.

Canon William Heygate,
Brighstone Banner of Faith, *March 1888*

Love

Arms outstretched – agony.
Head hung down – bleeding.
Ebbing life – once vibrant.
Rough cross – once a sheltering tree.
Irony.

Nails and thorns – cruel.
Side abused and weeping.
Heart broken and forsaken.
Mocked – yet spirit free.
Incredibly.

Ponder upon Gethsemane,
Betrayal in chilling air.
The carpenter who once hewed wood
Left hanging on the timbers bare.
His faith and overwhelming love
With all to share.
Shamelessly.

Christ for all,
Endured the gall,
He saved my soul.
You can believe
He died for thee
At Calvary.
Truthfully.

Pamela Georgina Debney

The price of love

Who shall ask the price of love?
Who shall assess the cost?
Who shall think to take account?
What's given, what is lost?

Richard J. Hutchings

Easter

Trust the English to be different from everyone else! The death and resurrection of Jesus was originally celebrated in a single event – the Paschal mystery, deriving its title from the Hebrew Passover – *Pesach*. In Greek and Latin this becomes *Pascha*, in Russian *Paskha*, in French *Paques*, Spanish *Pascua*, Italian *Pasqua*, even in Cornish it is *Pask*. In English, we speak about the Paschal mystery, referring to the great mystery of faith: Christ could not be contained by death, but rose again from the grave. The title, 'Easter', however, is derived from a Northern European, spring pagan festival, in honour of a Germanic dawn-goddess called 'Eostre'. It is probably fourteen centuries too late, but The Paschal Weekend is a much more appropriate name for this – the greatest of Christian Festivals.

This is the one festival which can be traced right back to the New Testament. 'Christ our Passover has been sacrificed for us,' writes St. Paul, 'so let us celebrate the feast'. It is the Resurrection that gives Christianity its defining message. Death is not the end. In a real sense, every Sunday is an Easter celebration, as we recall, week by week, the amazing news of the Resurrection. It was the reality of the Resurrection that gave the first disciples the confidence to stand up and proclaim their faith. We too have a message of good news to proclaim. Jesus offers new life, abundant life, to all who put their faith in him. To quote St. Paul again, 'If Christ has not been raised, your faith is futile . . . but Christ has indeed been raised from the dead, the first fruits of those who have fallen asleep . . . as in Adam all die, so in Christ all will be made alive' (from 1 Corinthians 15).

The natural colour for Easter, as the greatest festival of the year, is white, or gold.

But why then, such confusion every year concerning the date of Easter? It is an involved story. The original Paschal events occurred during the Passover Festival. Now the Passover always falls on the same date (the 14th Nissan), which, because Jewish months always begin with a new moon, is also the night of the full moon, although not necessarily on the same day of the week every year. The resurrection occurred on the first day of the week – symbolic as a sign of new life and new beginnings. So understandably, Christians wanted to celebrate these important events on the *first* day of the week. Therefore the celebration of Easter could not always coincide with the Passover. The Council of Nicea (AD 325) determined that Easter should be celebrated on the Sunday following the 14th day of the Paschal moon, which was decreed to be the first full moon following the vernal equinox. As the equinox is fixed upon 21st March, the consequence is that Easter Sunday can fall on the Sunday following the first full moon after 21st March, so it can fall any time between 22nd March and 25th April. This system for determining the date of Easter was adopted in England in AD 664, at the Synod of Whitby, when the official 'Roman' way of dating Easter was favoured over an alternative 'Celtic' system. Confused? Don't blame me – I'm only the messenger!

Dates aside, the important message of Easter is not *when* it is celebrated, but the truth of the Easter message.

The Lord is risen. He is risen indeed. Hallelujah!

Sunrise on Easter Day

Rise, rise, O sun, your glories bring,
Of light and heat: but lo! Your King
Has risen first with healing wing.

Wake herbs and flowers; the morning dew
Glitters with spring for ever new;
But most ye graves it shines on you.

Sing, O ye birds, your Easter lay,
And hail the ever-blessed day,
Whose joy can never pass away.

O all ye saints and angels sing,
And let the world with glory ring,
"Glory to risen Christ our King".

Canon William Heygate

A celebration

Celebrate Easter with New Life, not only in the garden, hedgerows and fields, but with new life in Jesus Christ. Don't just pass by the cross this year – look up and live!

Revd. Andrew Marke, curate,
Brighstone and District Newsletter, *1986*

From Lent to Easter

They only who have kept a penitent Lent can know the true joys of Easter – the joy of the heart risen from sin to the life of righteousness.

Canon William Heygate,
Brighstone Banner of Faith, *April 1890*

Hope

There can be little doubt we live in a world which needs the Easter message – of new life, new hope. God is the only hope. He's calling all of us to turn to Him. That's what the Easter message is all about.

Revd. Tim Eady,
Brighstone and District Newsletter, *May 1993*

At Easter

With bunnies, eggs and chocolate treats,
Commercial men a fortune seek!
Do they remember as they plan
What they were told when they were young?
That HE who came to save mankind
Was crucified at Easter time.
Or do they merely count the gain
In worldly wealth that they obtain?
Let us consider springtime flowers,
That gladden all our waking hours;
To find Easter exemplifies

Rebirth – as promised – so our lives
May have real meaning here on earth,
We too may have another birth.

Jack Camps

Easter Communion

On Easter Day from the earliest times of Christianity, the disciples have met together to witness to their belief in the risen Saviour, to remember his death for us on the cross, and to receive Him into ourselves in the form of bread and wine instituted by Him on the night of His betrayal. For these reasons the Church today has the same rule, that all who are Confirmed receive Holy Communion on Easter Sunday.

Revd Ralph Charlton,
Brighstone Parish Church News Sheet, *April 1965*

The Butterfly

The Butterfly goes round and round the garden in
    the sun,
It flutters here and flutters there, as if it's having fun.
It doesn't seem to really mind its unsteady, swerving
    gait,
But seems to enjoy its habit of never flying straight.

Jessie Booth

Low Sunday

"The morning after the night before" – a phrase guaranteed to conjure up a gloomy picture. A great time was had by all, but now is the time to get back to normal. The party is over. Perhaps that is why the Sunday after Easter is known as Low Sunday – not the morning after, but the Sunday after the Sunday before. It stands in sharp contrast to the 'high' feast of Easter.

In reality, Easter does not just finish. Our celebration of the Resurrection continues throughout the year – that is the prime reason for the transfer of the Christian holy day from the Jewish Sabbath, the seventh day of the week, to the day of resurrection, the first day of the week. Further, the season of Easter lasts for fifty days, until the Feast of Pentecost, mirroring the Great Fifty Days between Passover and Pentecost in the Jewish year. For the Jews this 'in between time' is a period of waiting, which designates the time between their deliverance from Egypt and the crossing of the Red Sea, to the giving of the law to Moses on Mount Sinai. For the Christian, this is a fifty day festival, which recognises the culmination of the promise of redemption in the Resurrection of Christ, and prepares us with joyful expectation for the celebration of the gift of the Holy Spirit at Pentecost. So Low Sunday should rightly be a time for recognition. The euphoria of the resurrection continues into a second week as we remember Thomas, the doubting one, who, a week after the other disciples, saw the risen Lord for himself and exclaimed 'My Lord and my God.'

We can learn something from the traditional Roman Catholic title for this day: Quasimodo Sunday – not because they venerate hunch backed bell ringers, but because Quasi modo are the first two words of the Latin mass for the day. Translated, the opening text of the mass reads, 'like new born babes you should thirst for milk, on which your spirit can grow to strength.' There's an apposite thought. A week into the season of resurrection, we should seek for spiritual strength – a good anti-thesis to the thought that the day is low.

Rogation Sunday

The fifth Sunday after Easter marks the second great agricultural festival of the year. Rogation comes from the Latin verb, rogare, to ask. This is a day to ask for God's blessing on the newly sown crops. In medieval times, it was an occasion on which to 'beat the bounds of the parish', an important way of instilling awareness of the community's territorial responsibilities into the younger generation by beating the boundary stones, or even beating young boys against the boundary stones – a custom which clearly predates our modern child protection laws!

In 21st century British society, where awareness of the agricultural seasons has become for so many of us of only secondary importance, Rogation Sunday offers an opportunity to remember our dependence upon the annual cycle of seedtime and harvest, without which, none of us could survive, and to pray with humble thanksgiving, for God's amazing provision as the bare earth once again breaks into blossom and new life. Coming as it does, at the very beginning of the summer season, this is also a day to pray for God's blessing upon our homes and community, as we recognise our dependence upon Him.

A prayer for the parish

Almighty God, we thank you for our parish,
and ask that you will be present in all that takes
    place
within its boundaries.

Give wisdom to those with responsibility
for making decisions which affect our corporate life.

Inspire with your Holy Spirit
those who care for our physical,
mental, and spiritual needs.
Grant comfort and healing to any
who are in trouble, sickness or distress.

And direct our ways
so that we may prepare ourselves
for the coming of your kingdom
and live as servants of our Living Lord,
Jesus Christ. Amen.

Revd. Tim Eady

Community

The importance of a place: walking along the Downs
reminded me that we need a sense of belonging. Restless-
ness is a feature of modern man's life. I thank God daily
that I know that I am where God has placed me, and that I
live in a community where I belong.

Canon Stephen Palmer,
Brighstone and District Newsletter, *1985*

May

There's a blossom on the cherry,
The plum and apple too,
A promise of the harvest,
That ripens summer through.

The grass is so much greener,
The hedges white with thorn,
The birds rejoice and carol,
A chorus to the dawn.

Peggy Thompson

Ascension

Falling as it does on a Thursday, Ascension Day is one of those festivals that can easily be overlooked, even by the faithful. It marks the event, forty days after the resurrection, when Jesus publicly and visibly parted with his disciples to return to His Father, with instructions for them to remain in Jerusalem until they received the Holy Spirit. It is an event that had to happen. Jesus couldn't simply go on appearing to his followers indefinitely. There had to be a cutting off point, after which they must get on with the mission that He had entrusted to them.

What is significant in St. Luke's account of the Ascension is how he describes the disciples returning from the Mount of Olives 'with great joy'. Surely, after the departure of such a good friend, there would be, at least, an element of sadness. Curiously, this appears to be an event that precipitated a great burst of worship and praise, so there must have been something special about the Ascension that gave the disciples the assurance that the best was still to come.

Jesus had promised that when he left them, he would send the Holy Spirit to be with them. He had to go, in order to be with them in a more complete way. In human form, he was confined to one time and place, but through the presence of the Holy Spirit, he is no longer confined to the parameters of the physical world, but can be with all believers simultaneously, at all times and in all places. So the disciples waited in Jerusalem, not in sadness at the loss of a good friend, but in joyful expectation of God's presence with them. Jesus had described the Spirit as Counsellor, Comforter and Guide, hence the disciples were anticipating the joy of the presence of God that would remain with them permanently. The Ascension had to happen before the Holy Spirit could come. The Ascension demonstrably signifies the end of the earthly ministry of Jesus, and the beginning of the story of the Church. Jesus ascended in order that we, like the disciples, may receive His Holy Spirit. So, after Ascension Day, we also wait with eager expectation for the great day of Pentecost. We too can wait with expectation and great joy.

The celebration of Ascension day

Christ our Ascended Priest and King calls us up to himself in glory. Let us consider the Collect carefully, and try to act upon it. Let us not fail to draw near to him in that service in which it is said to us, 'Lift up your hearts', and let us answer with our affections and in our lives, 'We lift them up unto the Lord'. The long neglect of this great and happy day is surely passing away, and will seem strange to our children. Is it possible that we can love Christ? Is it possible that we can wish for heaven, and forget Him on that day on which He went up to His God and to our God, received His glory, and prepared a place for us, opening the kingdom of Heaven to all believers. No, we cannot. We cannot neglect this blessed day.

Canon William Heygate,
Brighstone Banner of Faith, *May 1888*

The mystery of the Ascension

The Ascension is and must remain a mystery. It is an attempt to put into words what is beyond description. Ascension Day is a dividing day. It was the day when the Jesus of earth finally became the Christ of heaven. It was the one final moment when Jesus did go back to the glory that was his from the beginning. Jesus who had come in a moment of time was to leave at a moment of time.

Canon Stephen Palmer,
Brighstone and District Newsletter, *May 1983*

Pentecost

It used to be a bank holiday weekend. Now the holiday seldom coincides so, despite being second in importance only to Easter itself, Pentecost, (or Whit weekend) gets forgotten by the world at large. Pentecost recalls the foundation event of the Christian Church. It is rightly known as the Church's birthday.

Let us take Whitsunday first. Like Easter, this is a peculiarly English name for the day. Literally, it means 'White Sunday', from the custom of using this festival as an occasion for baptism, when candidates would appear dressed in white clothes, as a symbol of purity. This custom has continued until recent times in the rite of Confirmation, when girls would wear white dresses. But Pentecost is the older, and more appropriate name for the day, which takes us right back to its origins. Literally, it means fifty, reminding us that Pentecost falls fifty days after Passover.

Jesus told his disciples to wait in Jerusalem, until the Holy Spirit came upon them. On the feast of Pentecost, we read the story in Chapter 2 of the Acts of the Apostles, in which the Holy Spirit came, affirmed them in their faith, filled them with His presence, and sent them out to proclaim the good news of Jesus Christ. The symbol for Pentecost is fire, representing the tongues of fire that touched those first disciples as the Holy Spirit came upon them, and symbolic also of the rapid spread of the gospel, like wildfire, across the Roman Empire.

Of course, Pentecost was first of all, a Jewish festival, within which a key factor was the celebration of the giving of the law to Moses on Mount Sinai. So it is no coincidence that God should use this feast as an occasion on which to give the Spirit to his followers. The Holy Spirit represents a new kind of law, no longer written on tablets of stone, but on the flesh of the human heart; no longer a series of commandments, but the law of the Spirit – primarily the law of love, which challenges us to consider our attitudes and behaviour. This is more than just a blind obedience to a series of laws. What really counts is obedience to God, and the extent to which we exhibit the fruit of His Spirit in our lives. Once again we must turn to St. Paul to learn precisely what these fruit are: love, joy, peace, patience, kindness, gentleness, self-control. These characteristics grow in us when we open ourselves up to the life of the Holy Spirit.

So Pentecost is a birthday celebration, but not just an occasion to look back and count up the years. It is a day to encourage us to deepen our commitment to God, by welcoming the Holy Spirit as ruler of our hearts and lives. The colour of the season is red, as we remember the tongues of fire which came to rest upon the heads of the disciples.

Whitsuntide

Most of us look upon our birthdays as days for rejoicing, days on which our dearest are gathered around us. Whit-Sunday is often called the birthday of the Church, and as such it should be a day that is very precious to all Christian hearts. It should make us think of the many, many priceless blessings which the Church enjoys through the coming of the Holy Ghost.

Canon William Heygate,
Brighstone Banner of Faith, *June 1897*

From Lent to Whitsun

During the six weeks of Lent we try to be more
  thoughtful
Of other's needs, and not our own, our daily
  pleasures to overrule,
Good Friday comes, and we feel sad, Jesus gave his all,
He died for us, for you and me, our backs against
  the wall.
Easter Day is joyous and known by everyone
Easter Monday is a holiday and all have lots of fun.

Our churches are filled with flowers and our Rector
  distributes eggs,
Our hymns and anthems are full of joy, the music is
  raised several pegs.
The bells ring out, families gather, and Easter egg
  hunts begin
The child who finds the most is the one who is
  cheered to win.
The break from school and work is enjoyed and time
  is spent together
Sometimes the sun shines, sometimes it is wet, cold
  and snowy weather.

The next Christian festival is Whitsun, but this is a
  quieter one
Whit Monday is no longer known, I remember the
  words of my Mum,
'On Whit Sunday you wear something white, a
  dress, a skirt or a hat',
Now not many know of Whitsun, or the story of a
  great fact

That the disciples were given powers to speak in
several tongues
To spread God's word of His great deeds and His
love for everyone.

Whit Monday is now Spring Bank Holiday, still a
day of no school or work,
But not connected to Whit Sunday – a great pity for
the 'Kirk'.
The festival of Whitsun was one of the greatest in the
Christian year,
Because it is becoming forgotten makes us shed a
tear,
But take care to remember why we have Spring Bank
Holiday,
And continue to love Jesus, on this day, and in every
way.

Anon, 2004

A Prayer for the Holy Spirit

O my God, Thou hast promised to give Thy Holy Spirit to
those that ask it. Behold Lord, I do humbly, I do earnestly,
ask Thy Holy Spirit now of Thee, O fulfil Thy gracious
promise to me, O vouchsafe me that Holy Spirit I pray for,
to purify my corrupt nature, to strengthen my weakness, to
comfort me in troubles, to support me in discouragements,
to succour me in temptations, and to assist me in all parts
of my duty, that I may ever hereafter live in Thy fear, and
in constant, sincere and universal obedience, to all Thy
righteous Laws.

Bishop Thomas Ken

Filled with the Spirit

How can we be sure that the Holy Spirit lives within us, today, here in Brighstone? By his hallmarks! His (for he is a person) hallmarks are manifest, first in the fruits of the Spirit – love, joy, peace, longsuffering, gentleness, goodness, faithfulness, meekness, temperance. The next hallmark of the Spirit is His power – the power to convict, to challenge, and to convert. The surrounding world was made uncomfortable by the convicting, converting power of the Holy Spirit filled fellowship of the early church. A third hallmark of the Holy Spirit is charity – dynamic, overflowing love breaking down all barriers of ecclesiastical cold shouldering, social snobbery, national and racial suspicion. Where the Holy Spirit is manifestly at work there is a passionate desire for unity, a restless seeking after truth, however painful and inconvenient it may be.

These marks of the Holy Spirit – joy, peace, His power to convict and convert, and above all, charity – dynamic, overflowing love – are these manifest in our Church, in our congregation? If they are, we have truly opened our hearts and minds to the Holy Spirit; if they are not, there are prayers to be said and hearts and minds to be opened this Whitsuntide – or sooner.

Revd. Gordon Broome,
Brighstone Newsletter, *June 1973*

Pentecost and preaching

The New Testament contains many accounts of sermons and preachers. The most extraordinary sermon of all was the one preached by Peter on the day of Pentecost. The heart of the uncompromising message was that Jesus was born, taught, wrought miracles, was crucified and was raised to life on the third day. Peter also said that Jesus will one day return in glory to establish his kingdom on earth. The sermon ended with the statement that Jesus was the exclusive and only way of salvation – of being right with God. This hard cutting edge to the first Christian sermon calls into question many of the sentimental platitudes that sometime come from present day pulpits. Swinburne, the Victorian poet who lived for a while at Shorwell, once accused a preacher that he had 'for their tender minds served up half a Christ'. This sermon also puts us on the spot and asks us how we have responded to God's good news – the Gospel of Jesus Christ.

Not only are we told the contents of the first Christian sermon, we are also told of its effects. Those listening were cut to the heart. They asked what they should do, and 3,000 people were baptized on that day. In other words, when Jesus Christ, crucified and risen, is preached in His Father's name by the power of the Holy Spirit, people respond. We should respond.

Canon Stephen Palmer,
Brighstone and District Newsletter, *July 1988*

I will not leave you comfortless

When the Holy Spirit is among men, Christ is there.
When the Holy Spirit is in the heart of men, Christ is there.
When the Holy Spirit moves the worshippers to meet and offer prayers in spirit and in truth, Christ is there in the midst of them.
Be sure of this: If any man hath not the Spirit of Christ, he is none of His.

But if any man hath the Spirit of Christ, Christ is
with him.
Not indeed in the flesh, as of old when He was with
the disciples in Judea,
But very truly, very really and very near.
For with the presence of the Spirit, Christ too comes,
yea, and the Father;
And they make their abode in the heart which the
sanctifying Spirit maketh fit for such holy inmates.

Bishop George Moberly,
Parochial Sermons, mainly from Brighstone

Love is the song

The greatest gift is love
Followed by understanding
Given with consideration
Wrapped in patience
    With no demanding.

Handled with care, concern,
Passed gently along,
Whispered, written, called,
Keep it safe for ever
    Love is the song.

Jessie Booth

Trinity Sunday

If you follow the Church's lectionary, Trinity Sunday is significant. All the Sundays for the next few months, up until the end
of October in fact, are numbered from this point. It is an
important day in its own right, and has been since 1334, when
Pope John XXII decreed its general observance.

The Trinity may be dismissed as a theological concept, of
interest to scholars and theologians, but bearing little rele-
vance to the daily outworking of our faith. Surely, living the
faith, in word and deed, is more important than making
dogmatic statements? Perhaps it is, but the Trinity is a helpful
means of enabling us to understand the character of God, and
relating to Him more easily. At one time, Trinity Sunday stood
as the culmination of the Christian year, completing the cycle
which begins in Advent, when we think about the relationship
between God and the world, continues through Christmas up
until Ascension, when we recall the significant events of
Christ's life, moves to Pentecost and the pledge of the Holy
Spirit, before reaching Trinity Sunday which puts all those
pieces together. We think about God as Creator, Redeemer
and Life-Giver. There are three sides to God's character but
one God; three ways of experiencing God, but one God; three
ways of relating to God, but one God. Out of all this come the
various symbols that help to explain it – the trefoil, the linked
circles, the triangle.

So, Trinity is not about abstract theology at all. Rather, it
offers a way of bringing us into relationship with God – the

God who created us; the God who died on the cross for our salvation; the God who comes to us today with life-giving power.

As a major festival, the colour for Trinity Sunday is white, but the following season of Trinity, which continues until the beginning of November, is green.

The Doxology

Praise God, from whom all blessings flow,
praise him, all creatures here below,
praise him above, ye heavenly host,
praise Father, Son, and Holy Ghost. Amen.

Bishop Thomas Ken

Trinity

My hand can hold perfection in a rose bud,
My fingers open with it as it blooms.

I do not ask of God to take a form -
I know my puny brain could never frame it -
I only pray that I may feel the presence,
and open petals to absorb the light.

My eyes can follow birds to the horizon.
Their destination is a hazy guess.

I do not stress to grasp eternity:
I read those thirty years of precious time,
Redemption came to earth in human form:
And take resurrection's mystery on trust.

From earth's four corners there blows in the wind
Sounding predictions in unwary ears.

When I begin to doubt my better judgement,
Then I remember that the Spirit rode in
On the great wings of the Pentecostal wind,
And I can flower with its unseen breath.

Elizabeth Heward Bowyer

The Baptism window

In our parish church, immediately to the east of the
doorway, there is a stained-glass window, illustrating a
very precious moment in our Lord's earthly life – His
baptism by John the Baptist. At the instant, our Lord felt
full of his vocation to be the Saviour of the world. The
window is, in effect, a picture of the Trinity, for here we
have the voice of the Heavenly Father, 'Thou art my Son,
my Beloved; on thee my favour rests', the presence of His
beloved Son, and the promptings of the gentle, dove-like,
Holy Spirit. Led by Jesus, and those who had known him,
this was how the earliest believers came to be aware of
God. He was a loving, caring Father; He came into their
individual and corporate life as a gracious Spirit; He had
been with them on earth as a Master, Lord and Deliverer.
Their mental picture from the banks of the Jordan made
sense to them because it was a kind of a colour photograph
of their own experience of God. Trinity Sunday reminds us
of the depth and richness of this Christian experience
which we share, or could share, with those first believers.

Revd. Gordon Broome,
Brighstone Newsletter, *May 1978*

The hills

Lift your eyes to the hills, my son,
To the craggy hills and the sky,
When the trees bend on prevailing winds
And the soaring curlews cry.

Your help will come from the hills, my son,
For peace and joy are there.
Let your heart sing with the birds, my son
And they will lift your care.

You may not climb to the hills my son,
You may not walk that way.
But you will not look in vain, my son,
At the start of every day.

Lift up your eyes to the hills, my son,
And in your heart a prayer.
Just ask for all the help you need,
The Lord is always there.

Peggy Thompson

The Weeks after Trinity

The long period of weeks following Trinity Sunday is classed as 'Ordinary Time'. It covers the entire summer, and concludes at the end of October. This time is "ordinary" in that there are no great feasts to celebrate. We have come to the end of the cycle of festivals which teach us about the life of Jesus. Now we must apply our faith to our lives. These are weeks in which to consider the implications of faith.

A personal letter

Suffer me to add what I think my father's life so beautifully shows, that a deep and increasing personal religion must be the root of that firm and unwearied consistency in right, which I have ventured thus to press upon you. May you in another walk, and in still higher opportunities of service, as perfectly illustrate the undoubted truth that those who honour Him, He will honour.

Letter from Samuel Wilberforce to W.E. Gladstone,
20th April 1838

The rainbow

What a beautiful sight a rainbow is
As it stretches across the sky
A vision of real beauty
Above us, way up high.

The colours change from the rich dark tones
To delicate shades, then fade,
Nothing on earth can compare with it
Or by man could be made.

Jessie Booth

Thomas Ken – June 8th

Thomas Ken, Rector of Brighstone 1667–1669, and later
Bishop of Bath and Wells, has his own feast day on June 8th.
Here is another local celebration that merits an entry in a
Brighstone Book of Seasons. No-one knows for certain where
he first penned his famous hymns, but they were probably
written whilst he was a young man, and all good Brisoners
know for certain that he was inspired whilst sitting beneath the
yew tree in the Rectory garden!

An evening hymn

Glory to thee, my God, this night
for all the blessings of the light;
keep me, O keep me, King of kings,
beneath thy own almighty wings.

Forgive me, Lord, for thy dear Son,
the ill that I this day have done,
that with the world, myself, and thee,
I, ere I sleep, at peace may be.

Teach me to live, that I may dread
the grave as little as my bed;
teach me to die, that so I may
rise glorious at the awful day.

O may my soul on thee repose,
and may sweet sleep mine eyelids close,
sleep that may me more vigorous make
to serve my God when I awake.

When in the night I sleepless lie,
my soul with heavenly thoughts supply;
let no ill dreams disturb my rest,
no powers of darkness me molest.

Bishop Thomas Ken

Sea Sunday – the second Sunday of July

Here in Brighstone, "Sea Sunday" is a well-established event, a day when we think and pray especially for all the good work of the Mission to Seamen. A seaman can be away from home for as long as nine months at a time. Imagine the loneliness, the boredom and mental stress this can mean. The Mission to Seamen is that part of the Church which sets out to help seafarers in the difficult circumstances which surround their way of life. The symbol by which the Mission is known, is the "Flying Angel", inspired by the Book of Revelation, Chapter 14: 6 – look it up!

Revd. Gordon Broome,
Brighstone Newsletter, *July 1977*

A Brighstone summer

The choral society has given a most successful concert. The villagers came in crowds, labourers hurrying in from the hayfields to be in good time. . . . Fortunately we have had glorious weather for the last fortnight, and the garden is looking perfect with all the white lilies in bloom. Yesterday, we walked to Brook along the cliff. . . . The sea was the deepest purple and green against the red cliffs, and the seagulls floated upwards in flocks, crying and yapping as we passed. Ships are shy of our dangerous bay, and we do not see any beyond an occasional steamer on the extreme horizon. The great loneliness adds a grandeur to our sea. Nothing disturbs the gulls and the cormorants. From the Downs there is a sort of opalescent colouring over sea and sky, owing to our being on an island.

Catherine A.E. Moberly, July 1869
Quoted in Dulce Domum

A 19th century pursuit – the other side of seafaring

Until the last decade of the century (the 19th) an added income for fishermen came from smuggling. It is written that this was not regarded as an antisocial activity, just a manner of supplementing income – earning an honest penny! Plus, the excitement of 'doing' the coastguard. The chief traffic was brandy, usually obtained from Barfleur or Cherbourg. The first part of the programme was to obtain the money to buy the cargo. Sometimes, the men would raise some between themselves, but most of it came from the farmers, doctor and parson. The men of the shore party were a very essential part of the proceedings. They had to be utterly reliable, and obtain information on the movements of the coastguards, or arrange to bribe them, and also be ready to unload and hide the cargo when it arrived. They helped to carry the tubs up the cliff and stowed them in their hiding places to be retrieved in due course. The tubs cost about fourteen shillings each and the freight charge was three shillings each. The shore hands received three shillings and sixpence for each one safely landed.

There were four gallons of proof spirit in each, which was diluted with the same quantity of water and colouring matter made with burnt sugar was added. The eight gallons were then each sold for two pounds ten shillings or in pint bottles for two shillings and sixpence a pint. The demand always exceeded the supply.

Dorothy Brooke,
from Brighstone in the Nineteenth Century

Summer pursuits

July is to English people the month of parish outings. Day by day from the hot and sultry streets of London, men or mothers, children or elder girls, and lads, are being carried in trains, full to overflowing, out for a 'day in the country'. Only those who have spent part of their lives hemmed in by miles of dull brick houses can appreciate the intense joy that these words imply. We, living in this happy and beautiful village, do not need such a change as they do, but some outing is good for all of us, and we, as a parish, take part in this general fashion.

Revd. Ernest Silver,
Brighstone Banner of Faith, *July 1903*

Village social life

The creation by the curate, the Revd. A. C. Baker of a Reading Room in 1880 gave an opportunity for seeing local and national newspapers and also some magazines. . . . Residents paid sixpence a month to be members. An expenditure of fourteen shillings on entertainment and one pound eighteen shillings and ten pence on a lecture on 'Egypt' show that reading was not the only pursuit. In the

Annual Report it was emphasised that lady members would be welcome, and could use the premises before 6 p.m.

The bell ringers constituted another group of men who met weekly to practice and ring, and enjoyed an annual outing and other social events. They had a somewhat severe set of rules which included the prohibition of any drink in the tower except water and a fine for swearing of one shilling for the first offence, two shillings for the second offence and expulsion for the third.

Towards the end of the century a Cottage Garden Show was begun and appears to have had considerable success from its inception. A particularly enjoyable day was always reported.

The Girls' Friendly Society flourished as did the Cricket Club, the Church Choir, the Church of England Temperance Society, evening classes in the winter, sacred concerts and special events to raise funds for whatever cause had been brought to the attention of the villagers. National events were noted and the Jubilee of Queen Victoria was marked with a dinner in the school room, tea in the nearby field with music from the band of the Isle of Wight Rifles, and a Grand Finale of a bonfire on the Downs in the evening. In all, a picture of a community which was increasingly active and characteristically rural.

Dorothy Brooke,
from Brighstone in the Nineteenth Century

Lammas Day

August 1st – Lammas Day, brings us to the third of the four historic agricultural festivals. Alongside Harvest, this is the most biblically based of the festivals. Lammas Day corresponds to the Old Testament Feast of the First Fruits – the day on which a sheaf of the first grain of the harvest was brought to the priest to be offered to the Lord. In Leviticus 23, this day is the day after the first Sabbath following the Passover, the day of our Lord's resurrection, hence Christ is described as 'the first fruits of those who have fallen asleep' (1 Cor 15:20).

Of course, the British climate is very different from the eastern Mediterranean, and so Lammas Day falls later in the year than its Jewish forebear. It is historically a day for the offering of the first fruits of the English harvest. The precise origins of the day are lost in the shrouds of time, but there is documentary evidence of its use as early as the reign of King Alfred the Great. Traditionally, it was the day on which the first bread to be baked from the year's harvest was brought to the church and used for the Eucharist. The word Lammas is a contraction of Loaf-mass.

So, as the harvest season gets underway, Lammas is a day to remind ourselves that we should never take the fruits of the earth for granted, but give thanks to God, and in keeping with His generous nature, we too must remember the importance of being generous with our bounty and sharing it with others in need.

Midsummer's Day

To lie beneath a summer sky,
With deep soft meadow as my bed;
To scent the dewy cups on high,
And hear grass whispering 'round my head.

A skylark singing at its height,
And bees attending every flower;
The cuckoo calls while in her flight;
Would that her signal still the hour.

This very Sun which lights the Earth,
With changing days from end to end;
O'er torrid wastes and frozen dearth,
Smiles down on England as a friend.

Leslie V. Hall May 1998

Morning is breaking

Now is the time to listen to
the songbirds singing just for you.
Now is the time to listen to
their early throng in the morning.

This is the time to sit and watch
as the daylight comes and the world is still
the air is fresh, the world tranquil.
It is just for you in the morning.

Now is the time for you and for me
to count the dew drops, one, two, three,
as the sun breaks through and the day begins

when the lark and the thrush so joyously sing,
first things first in the morning.

It is six o clock, the trees are still,
the pond is too . . .
what a wonderful time to just be here
to catch the scene of a world asleep,
Such a peaceful time in the morning.

The day is here, the world awake
the sounds of people, as they breakfast make,
their voices echo, the birds disappear,
the traffic moves for all to hear . . .
Was I dreaming it all in the morning?

Margo Perks

Ssh listen

Summer seas, rolling over rich golden sands,
Fill pure pools, cupped like mermaids hands
Run rippling restive over purring stones,
Making rhapsodies of restless tones.
Rolling, rippling, sea washed shells,
Singing summer seas, weave summer spells.

Tumbling tresses of sea tossed wrack,
Bone white shells on the shores ridged back.
Wind whispering through the leaves,
Like ladies lovely silken sleeves.
Green sea, white waves, blue sky,
Seagulls mewing up on high.

Paula Woodford

Look and see

The world is full of beauty, it surrounds and enfolds
man,
Look and see, enjoy it all, watch it while you can,
The wonder of each day that dawns, the stillness of
the night,
All the beauty of the earth, is here within your sight.

Clouds that sail in skies of blue, a rainbow way up
high,
The sunrise and the sunset, streams and rivers
flowing by,
Butterflies, birds and bees, and wonderful to see,
Each one special and unique, as it was meant to be.

Mountains reaching way above, valleys down below,
Fields that go for miles and miles, divided by
hedgerow.
Living things that move and breathe, big ones and
the small,
All are given life to live, earth's treasures are for all.

This perfect planet all for us, with wonders
everywhere,
Inspiring pictures, song and verse, from people
moved to care,
We live among such magic, mere mortals as we are,
Let us now review ourselves, observe things near
and far.

Don't wish that you had noticed, when it becomes
  too late,
This world so full of beauty, who knows if it can
  wait.

Jessie Booth

Harvest Festival

And so we come to Harvest Festival, one of the most popular, and best celebrated of all feasts and seasons. Like Lammas Day, it dates back as far as Saxons times. The Old Testament parallel is the Feast of the Tabernacles, celebrating the in-gathering of the threshing floor and wine press. However, in its present form, harvest celebrations have much to do with their popularisation during Victorian times. Perhaps because of growing urbanisation, the annual harvest decoration of churches with the reminder of our dependence upon God's bounty, achieved a new significance.

Our present traditions can be traced to the 1840s, in the church of Morwenstow on the beautiful, but bleak, north Cornish coastline. The vicar, the Revd. Robert Hawker, was renowned as a great lover of animals and the countryside, and was most likely inspired by the poverty of the farmers and labourers around him, and awareness of the importance of a good harvest for their welfare. So, with a suitably decorated church, he established the custom of a service of thanksgiving for a safe and successful harvest.

Today, food production has become the preserve of a few specialists. Most of us never get beyond the supermarket shelves, but in pre-20th century times a poor harvest could mean a whole winter of austerity, and even starvation. Everything depended upon a good harvest. Hawker's idea of decorating the church with fruit and vegetables rapidly caught on, until Harvest Festival became something of a national institution.

This is a festival which reminds us of the importance of thanksgiving, and not just to take the world for granted, so it is appropriate that in recent years, in many urban parishes, prayers of thanksgiving have been included, not only for the harvest of the land, but for the harvest of industry, and all the commodities which provide us with our quality of life. It is also a useful reminder of the importance of exercising Christian stewardship of the environment. We have been given dominion over the world, but ultimately, it belongs to God, and to Him we will be answerable.

A harvest celebration

Mrs and Miss Yonge have been staying here, and during their visit Brighstone had its Harvest Thanksgiving Service. We spent the afternoon wreathing the church with scarlet geraniums and brilliant flowers, and Miss Yonge undertook to make the double triangle of grapes and corn for the east end; our helpers were greatly interested to see her with her dress tucked up sweeping out the chancel with a long-handled broom. The church was thronged; nearly everyone in the place must have come to the service, and at the end the bells rang merrily. Before coming in we ran down the garden through the soaking grass to see the moon rise large and red.

Catherine A.E. Moberly, September 1867
Quoted in Dulce Domum

Thanksgiving

On Tuesday September 25th, we kept our Parish Church Harvest Festival. May the large congregation in the beautifully decorated church, the hearty singing of choir and people, and the pealing bells, truly represent our abiding feeling of thankfulness to Almighty God for the many benefits which He daily pours down upon us in this place.

Revd. Ernest Silver,
Brighstone Banner of Faith, *October 1906*

Words of Harvest

> Within the word of HARVEST
> Many words are found
> So just like all the seasons
> Now lets turn those letters round.
>
> At HARVEST time we think of food
> Ripe golden corn and EARS of wheat
> Especially of our daily bread
> So good for us to EAT.
>
> Such wondrous things within our world
> Should make our HEARTS feel glad
> Yet nations STARVE – they have no food
> This makes us, oh – so sad.
>
> We must not let the hungry STARVE
> Or TEARS we'll surely shed
> Invite the needy home for TEA
> And let them REST instead.
>
> Within the word of HARVEST
> Is just the word we need
> If only we could learn to SHARE
> We'd forget our selfish greed.

Within the word of HARVEST
So many words there are
Let's SHARE the many gifts we HAVE
We'll each then be a STAR.

Michael Camps

Children's Harvest

We used to help with the harvest and one time I was at
Grange Farm and we loaded the wagon up with corn and
then went with it for a ride to Compton. On the way back
we all fell asleep and they had to wake us up and send us
home. It was so late I got into trouble when I got home. We
also used to follow the binder as it cut the corn. The rabbits
would all run out and we used to chase them, trying to
catch them. If we caught one we got 3d. for it, so that meant
extra pocket money for sweets.

Rob Snow,
recalling his childhood

September

The leaves begin to turn
A lovely shade of gold.
Red apples in the orchard,
Soft breeze across the World.

The harvest nearly over –
The golden fields are gone,
and misty moist mornings
Greet the coming dawn.

Peggy Thompson

Autumn

Autumn has come – smell the air!
She has caught us unaware.
Lovely she comes with gold-rimmed cloud.
Yet softly, imperceptibly
She paints the trees with sparkling gilt,
With jocund wind and jewel-like rain
With frosted breath she cools and glows.

Richard J. Hutchings

Age

The patience of the gentle old
Is like the lovely hidden gold,
There for those who care to seek
Their company, Blessed are the meek.

We who are young need to be told
About this lovely hidden gold,
That we may pray each in our turn,
If we will take the time to learn.

Paula Woodford

The seaside in October

The fallen leaves stir
And flee down the street,
The dead leaves of summer
A thousand ghost feet.
Now low'ring mists hang
And gone are the swallows.
The sea air is chilling

Too soon winter follows.
And gone are longshoremen –
No trips round the bay.
Off with the merchant fleet
East to Malay.
The hotels are empty
Their owners in Spain.
Flown are the golden geese,
South from the rain.

Time heavily drags
The long winter through
When comforts are cold
And pleasures are few.
Then what do we do?
No doubt you have guessed:
Thank God for small mercies,
Be glad of the rest.

Richard J. Hutchings,
(written after a busy season in his shop in Shanklin)

Home is where the heart is

Home is where the heart is, where future dreams are
    born,
Where folk are filled with joyous hearts,
    And sometimes hearts are torn.

Home is where the heart is, the people – how they
    live,
Children with their Mums and Dads and all the love
    they give.

A photograph of Grandmama and dear old Grandpa
    too
Bring memories back of yesteryear to link with
    friends anew.

Home is where the heart is, that dear old crippled
    man
Surrounded by such treasures that reflect his long
    life's span.

As the clock upon the mantle-shelf in measured
    minutes ticks
Tells old age is creeping up on you, for walking
    needs both sticks!

When young we love to wander, now no longer need
    to roam,
As absence makes the heart grow fonder for that
    place called 'home'.

Home is not mere bricks and tiles with windows
    double glazed,
Nor roses round a quaint front door led to by
    pathway crazed.

But 'Home is where the heart is', where you curl up
    by the fire
And look toward the future when at peace you can
    retire!

Michael Camps

Bible Sunday

It used to be lost in the midst of Advent, but now is more sensibly celebrated at the end of October. Bible Sunday offers an occasion to remember and give thanks for the gift of Holy Scripture. The theme of the day is well summarised in its Collect:

> Blessed Lord,
> who caused all Holy Scriptures to be written for our learning:
> help us so to hear them,
> to read, mark, learn, and inwardly digest them,
> that, through patience, and the comfort of your holy word,
> we may embrace and for ever hold fast the hope of everlasting
>   life,
> which you have given us in our Saviour Jesus Christ.

The Bible remains the authoritative book of the Christian Church. Whilst other books and authors are read, quoted, and labelled 'classics', the Bible alone is credited with being 'divinely inspired'. It has a place in public worship and private devotion, and still holds pride of place when it comes to Christian teaching.

It is fitting that one Sunday should be set aside to pay due respect to the place of Scriptures within our faith, and late October has been chosen because of its association with Martin Luther and the Reformation.

The question of the Sadducees

There is a great deal more depth of meaning in Holy Scripture than we of ourselves should be able to find in it. . . . But when the Lord Himself, Whose is the Holy Spirit which guided the pen of the writers of the Bible, comes to interpret these words, see what a wonderfully greater depth and richness of meaning they are seen to have than we could have found in them!

Bishop George Moberly,
Parochial Sermons, mainly from Brighstone

The Kingdom Season

The month of November contains various celebrations that direct our thoughts towards the fellowship of all believers, and the hope of eternal life. It begins with All Saints' Day, swiftly followed by All Souls Day, before moving on to remember the Saints and Martyrs of England, and then, Remembrance Sunday – always the second Sunday of November, being the closest Sunday to Armistice Day (November 11th). The culmination of these "end time" festivals is the Feast of Christ the King on the Sunday before Advent. In the most recent Church of England Prayer Book (Common Worship 2000), a composite name has been given to this period – "The Kingdom Season", thus providing a fitting conclusion to the Christian year, with a reminder of our mortality, and directing our thoughts heavenwards. Beyond death there is life, and over all is Christ the King, Lord of time and eternity, who has conquered death, and inaugurated the kingdom of God, thereby creating a unity between this life, and the life to come.

The colour of the Kingdom Season is red, primarily to recall the blood of the many Christian martyrs.

The kingdom

They crowned a Prince
Since
They didn't risk a King
Until he'd learned a thing
Or two –

And who,
They said, shall be his tutors?
Why, us indeed, they all agreed,
Or else he will not suit us.

They lent him a throne
And a gold-plated pen:
And then
They told him, You're a fine figure-head.
We'll rule in your stead:
Just sign on the dot,
We know what's what.

The prince grew in stature alone
On his throne.
He saw evil corrupt
And anger erupt
Till flames of war spread
Over innocent dead
Then he laid by his crown.

He stepped down –
He sought for the poor in the alleys of ruin,
He opened the door of compassion and drew in

Humanity's remnants, and said:
'Let us bury the dead –
There's a new world to build,
Let us labour together'.

So they crowned him a King –
To be killed.

Elizabeth Heward Bowyer

The presence of God

All things in earth and air
Are marvellous and fair,
    For Thou art there.

Joyful thy worship is.
Foretaste of endless bliss,
    For Thou art there.

But heaven is far more fair,
Lovely beyond compare,
    For Heaven's God is there.

Canon William Heygate

Take time

A time in our hearts to stop and be still,
To open our hearts for His goodness to fill,
A time to be thankful for friends that we know,
A time to give thanks for the kindness they show,
A time to be sad that we cannot still share,
The good things around us with people who care,

A time to speak out, to sing and rejoice,
A time to just listen to our own inner voice,
A time to be pensive – at one with our thoughts,
When needful of guidance, His help we have sought,
A time to rejoice in the mysteries of life,
With all of its sufferings, its struggles and strife,
In faith, hope and love, no good is concealed,
In fullness of time – His will is revealed.

Michael Camps

The sunset

Softly stealing across the sky
In shades of red and gold,
A sight to take the breath away,
So lovely to behold.

The clouds around are white and grey
Yet tinged with a golden glow,
They move at will across the sky
As on their way they go.

A memory to treasure,
A perfect picture seen,
The sunset in the evening sky,
An awe-inspiring scene.

Who could paint such magic,
Capture such delight,
Give such thought and detail
To the sky at night?

The wonder and the beauty
As the sunset slips away,
Will linger long when it has gone
And night takes over day.

Jessie Booth

Things seen

I am riding, for instance, on an old pony up a high hill. All at once the pony, no doubt smelling the salt of the sea, breaks into a canter of his own accord. I see, resting on green grass, brown leaves of autumn, grey rabbits scuttling for shelter from the bright golden spaniel who persistently pursues them in spite of countless failures. And in the distance is the glory of the brilliant blue sea with its waves breaking white far out from the shore, for it is low tide. Then there is the chalky white of the limestone cliffs: the deep green of the dell below; the vivid dark red of an old tiled roof; the greyish white of a flock of sheep. All this bursts upon the eye as you come over the top of the hill, and unless your soul be dead it will leap for joy at this glorious beauty.

But – with deep respect to my readers – here is the point on which I would insist. Whether you are riding a pony or walking on foot, or even – although I know this is much more difficult – driving in that dull thing, a motor car, stop still and keep on looking so long as you can enjoy the beauty that you see. Lower your eyes again to the ground, remember what you have seen, then look again and yet again, and say: "Well, I shall never forget that." If you look long and carefully, as the Greek word describes, believe me, there will be for you a perpetual joy; and when you are in your lodging in some big town, in the cold of winter, and the discomfort of the crowd, you can close your eyes and see again that wondrous scene which charmed your soul many months before. Nothing can rob you of that memory.

General Jack Seely, The 1st Lord Mottistone,
from Paths of Happiness

All Saints' and All Souls' Days (November 1st and 2nd)

The first two days of November offer the opportunity to remember the continuity that we share with all God's people of all times and places. We do more than simply remember those who have gone before us, we recognise that we too, are a part of the 'great cloud of witnesses' (Hebrews 12), who are called to testify to the greatness of God. Death is but a gateway to a greater realisation of life – "life in all its fullness" (John 10:10). The saints are not just holy people from the past, but all God's people of all times and all places, all who confess that Jesus Christ is Lord. All Saints' Day is a fitting occasion to remember the example of those who have gone before us, but we should do so as a way of encouraging ourselves to follow in their example, and to live our lives in a way that is honouring to God.

All Souls' Day has a subtly different emphasis from All Saints'. This is a day on which to thank God for the lives of the recently departed – those who we ourselves have known and loved, but who have gone before us. We thank God for all that they have taught us, and for the precious gift of memory, through which we can share in the good times of the past.

Diary entry

May the utter darkness of my life which can never be
dispelled kill in me all ambitious desires and earthly
purposes: my love of money and power and place, and
make me bow meekly to Christ's yoke.

Samuel Wilberforce, March 1841,
written the day after the death of his wife, Emily

All Saints' sermon

The thought of All Saints is a lofty and an elevating
thought. We know and we rejoice to know, that the souls of
the dead – the souls of those who have died in repentance
and faith – are in the hands of God. We delight to think of
them. We do not grieve, as men without hope or faith, if
those who are very near and dear to us are called away
from our side to join them. We delight to think that if our
company grows thinner upon earth, our store in Paradise
grows richer and fuller.

Christ is the Way, and repenting of our sins, and putting
our whole trust in His mercy for pardon and acceptance,
we shall not fail in our own due time to reach that happy
place where He led the soul of the penitent thief on the
Crucifixion day, and where we believe the souls of the
faithful, now delivered from the burden of the flesh, wait in
joy and felicity for the final triumph of the Judgement Day.

Bishop George Moberly,
Parochial Sermons, mainly from Brighstone

Roland's song

Brighstone nestled low beyond the down
Chalk faced, tree topped shelter from the northern
    wind;
In summer, sheep grazing
In winter, white wool snow lies thick in fleecy
    furrows,
Boys toboggan
White smoke curls a lazy finger round a red
    December sun.

Grey church tower and stubby spire
Stand in timeless affirmation of the faith of
    worshippers,
Singing praises to their Lord.

Roland sang for more than seventy years,
Sitting in an oaken stall,
Shoulder to shoulder with other men and boys
Who came, sang a shrill verse and then moved on.
Roland sang long and sweet,
Praising the Lord in slow deliberate harmony.

Born under the thatch,
With road, now tarmac, winding by.
Cabbage patch, green with leaf life,
Potato, sprouts, sweet smelling briar.
Earth set between the heel.
Fingers strong, as only hands of country men are
    strong.

Turning ancient hymns,
Wrestling with notes too high,
Or caught between the anthem and the psalm.

Roland sings a new song now
High notes echo and ebb,
Swelling like the sea,
Falling with thunder round the rocks.
Stilling into myriad pools of shining calm,
Sparkling into rivulets tracing through the sand,
As sweet harmony flows through the soul of
  peaceful man.

He died under the thatch.
The shell is finished and empty lies upon the sand
A vacant stall still vibrates with seventy years of
  song –
Roland's gone
To sing no doubt some heavenly round.
And when a new voice is found
When there's no gap in the oaken stall
Roland's voice will still be singing with us all.

Revd. Derick Stevenson,
written upon the death of faithful chorister
Roland Downer, in 1979

The silence of worship

Silence reigns, silence of prayers passed,
Silence, yet the loving prayers last,
Within these quiet walls, rough hewn

Lie depths of prayer like palm leaves strewn.
Now while the silence reigns the shadowed deeps
Seem full of the peaceful praying dead asleep.

The choir sings, the prayers rise,
Joined to past prayers, wise.
Loving God, we offer what we have to give,
Joys, sorrows, prayers, and the life we live.

Paula Woodford

Remembrance Sunday

Although not strictly a festival of the Christian year, Remembrance Sunday continues to hold a deep poignancy. As the great wars of the 20th century recede into history, this is a day upon which we remember all the victims of warfare, and those who made the ultimate sacrifice in order that we may live in peace and freedom. Whether it is because the reality of war is as great today as it ever has been, or whether it is purely respect for those who have gone before, the reality is that it is not only old soldiers, but many young people, who wish to show their respect on this day. It is an interesting fact that Remembrance Sunday congregations continue to remain large, and that many people whose sole experience of war is from history books wish to mark this day. As we remember the past, we pledge ourselves to work as peacemakers, and pray that the day will come when swords will be beaten into ploughshares.

Newsletter November 1990

All authority and power belong ultimately to God . . . and true peace can only come from obedience to God's plan for mankind.

Remembrance Sunday teaches us a similar lesson; it is a time of solemn reflection and re-dedication. It is a time for confession for the sins of mankind and a renewed commitment to work for justice and peace. Remembrance Sunday is a time for looking back – both in thanksgiving and sorrow – and also to look forward. We should pray earnestly for all world leaders, that they will devote themselves to the cause of peace and harmony within and between nations. . . . We do not do the memory of the glorious dead any honour if in our public expressions of gratitude for their sacrifice we ourselves are not at the same time prepared to pray, strive and work for peace.

Canon Stephen Palmer,
Brighstone and District Newsletter, *November 1990*

Three graves

Gloriously borne to the dust,
Tales of all faceless men have passed
Into oblivion, where a name alone
Brings grief to a womb which bore a son.
And as cider apples ripen and fall
By the side of the fathomless well,
In my heart they fall, I know,
That other seeds may live and grow.
Three graves moulded of alien soil,
Three men whose principles embroil
Them, cannot recall them to lands
Which extend their hopeful, grateful hands.
I cannot weep, but am ashamed.
That I fear for the courageous unfamed
For they knew the hour when men would say,
"Thank God that agony's black abyss has passed
    away."

Richard J. Hutchings,
(written on 8th August 1944, in memory of three soldier
colleagues, killed whilst defusing landmines in northern France)

For what?

Our young hope died!
Mother's, wives and sisters cried.
Our young hope died
In hope that peace would come to stay,
Even though they went away.
All giving of their ripe young life,
In hope that this would stop the strife.
Where is the peace for which they died?
The world is still a world too wide.
So men still fight
Losing life, limbs and sight
In hope that seems all hopelessness.
While children cry and die in loneliness,
The young hope died.
All for the worldly stubborn pride.

Paula Woodford

Christ the King (Stir Up Sunday)

Just as the Christian life should continue to grow upwards, in ever increasing circles, towards God, so too, each season of the Christian year flows naturally into the next. The weeks of the Kingdom lift our minds heavenwards, and remind us that we live with the tension between the kingdom of this earth, and the kingdom of heaven, ultimately reminding us that we look forward to the day when the Kingdom of God will be made visible, and Christ will be revealed as King over all kings. For now, just as Christ is God incarnate – fully human yet also fully divine, with no contradiction or division between the two, we too are called to live as members of two kingdoms – the Kingdom of God, and as responsible members of human society, the kingdom of this world. In short we must be both earthly and heavenly minded. This is well expressed in the BCP Collect for the last Sunday before Advent:

> Stir up, O Lord the wills of Thy faithful people,
> that plenteously bearing the fruit of good works,
> they may by Thee be plenteously rewarded;
> through Jesus Christ our Lord. Amen

This is a prayer that God will motivate us to right living, which will enable us to live out our faith in a way which is both honouring to God and which will demonstrate His love for the world around us. The theme is echoed in the Letter of James, which speaks of 'faith without works' being dead. Hence the traditional name for the day (not to mention the traditional activity – stirring Christmas puddings): Stir Up Sunday.

And so, with Stir Up Sunday, and thoughts of Christ the King, our minds turn once again to the coming of the King, as we prepare to celebrate Advent and to begin afresh the cycle of the Christian year. One year flows naturally into another, but we ourselves will be different. We take with us all that we have learned and experienced and now must apply it to a deeper understanding of what lies before us. Amidst the ever changing years, the one constant is God. "Jesus Christ the same, yesterday, today and forever" (Hebrews 13). We look towards the future with faith, hope, love, and certainty. With God, there always is a future.

My day

> It's been an awful day today,
> Fact is, it's not been my week –
> The car has had a puncture,
> The roof has sprung a leak.
> The ring's gone on the cooker,
> The dryer just won't spin,
> The dog has dug the garden –
> You can see the mess I'm in.
>
> Oh dear Lord, give me patience
> To face things as they come,
> To try to see the funny side,
> I'm better off than some.
> For there are those who have no shelter,
> No car, no roof to leak,
> No place to call their very own,
> No matter how they seek.

The world has turned against them,
A cold unfriendly place,
So, harder then to keep a smile,
And face the human race.

Help me O Lord, to be grateful,
And treasure what I've got,
To count my many blessings,
And be thankful for my lot.

Peggy Thompson

Winter arrives

This very wet season tells hardly on many: amongst others on the children who have to come from their homes to school over muddy roads and sometimes through slushy fields. It is very bad for their health that they should be sitting in wet feet all school time. To keep them as dry as possible, Mr. Lempriere wishes their parents to know that if they will send a spare pair of boots or shoes with them these shall be kept in the school: then the children can take off their wet boots when they come, and not put them on again till they need them for going home.

Revd E. Silver,
Brighstone Banner of Faith, *November 1903*

In Christ's steps

As oft, with worn and weary feet,
We tread earth's rugged valley o'er,
The thought – how comforting and sweet –

Christ trod this toilsome path before:
Our wants and weaknesses he knows,
From life's first dawning to its close.

Do sickness, feebleness, or pain,
Or sorrow in our path appear?
The sweet remembrance will remain –
More deeply did he suffer here.
His life, how truly sad and brief,
Filled up with sorrow, pain and grief.

If Satan tempt our hearts to stray,
And whisper evil things within,
So did he in the desert way,
Assail our Lord with thoughts of sin.
When worn and in a feeble hour,
The Tempter came with all his power.

Just such as I this earth He trod,
With every human ill but sin;
And though indeed the very God,
As I am now, so He has been.
My God, my Saviour, look on me,
With pity, love and sympathy!

Bishop Samuel Wilberforce

And Finally . . .

I give the last word to my favourite predecessor, Canon William Heygate. With him, I look forward to that day when 'time shall be no more', and we shall meet in glory.

A new century dawns

Our thoughts have been so much taken up with the war that it hardly seems possible to realise that a new century has dawned upon us. . . . It ought to be a very solemn time – a time for looking back and looking forward – a time for humiliation and penitence, for thanksgiving and for prayer, for humiliation and penitence because of our pride and manifold neglect, for thanksgiving because God has showered upon us such abundant mercies . . . for prayer that we may use God's mercy better in the future than we have done in the past, and that we may profit by the chastisement He has laid upon us.

More than this, dear friends, we will not say, except to send you our heartfelt "God bless you", now and in the coming years – for however much or however little of this new century you may see – and to express the wish that when time shall be no more we may meet again in the everlasting peace of God.

Canon William Heygate, Rector;
Revd. Leslie Knights Smith, Curate,
Brighstone Banner of Faith, *January 1900*

The Cloud of Witnesses

The Saints on Earth

Mr. John Ball, Head Teacher of Brighstone Primary School
    1961–1968

Mrs Jessie Booth

Mr Jack Camps

Mr. Michael Camps

Mrs Petrena Camps

Mrs Angela Clarke, Churchwarden of Mottistone
    1992–2001

Mr. Dennis Courtney, Head Teacher of Brighstone
    Primary School 1969–1982

Mr. Ivor Debney

Mrs Pamela Georgina Debney

The Revd. Timothy Eady, Rector of Brighstone, Brook and
    Mottistone, 1992–present

Mr Leslie V. Hall, former Deputy Harbour Master of
    Newtown Creek

Canon Stephen Palmer, Rector of Brighstone, Brook and
    Mottistone 1980–1991, now Vicar of Newport, Isle of
    Wight.

Mr. Christopher Parsonson

Miss Fiona Perks

Mrs Margot Perks

Mr. Robin Snow

The Revd. Derick Stevenson, now retired. *Roland's Song*
    written in 1979

Mrs Peggy Thompson

Mr. Robert Courtney Walker

Mrs Jean Wavell, Licensed Reader in the parishes of
Brighstone, Brook and Mottistone

The Revd. Paul Wilson, former Curate of Brighstone,
Brook and Mottistone

Mrs Susan Young

And those whose work is done

Mrs Elizabeth Heward Bowyer, wife of the Revd. Robert
Bowyer, Rector of Brook with Mottistone 1952–1978.
Poems reproduced by kind permission of the executors
of the Bowyer estate.

Miss Dorothy Brooke, eminent local historian. Died 2004.

The Revd. Gordon A. Broome, Rector of Brighstone
1972–1980, and Brook with Mottistone 1978–1980.

Mr. Robert Cassell, lifelong resident of Brook, died 2001.

The Revd. Ralph Charlton, Rector of Brighstone
1946–1972.

Miss Dorothy Cotton, lifelong local resident. Died 2002.

Canon William Heygate, Rector of Brighstone 1869–1903.

Mr. Richard J. Hutchings. Died 1991. Poems reproduced
by permission of Mrs Elizabeth Hutchings.

The Rt Revd. Thomas Ken, Rector of Brighstone
1667–1669, and later Bishop of Bath and Wells.

The Revd. Leslie Knights Smith, curate of Brighstone at
the turn of the 19th/20th century.

Mr. Rollo Denys Lempriere, son of a former Head Master
of Brighstone School. Died 2004.

The Revd. Andrew Marke, former Curate of Brighstone,
and later Chaplain with the Mission to Seafarers.
Died 2001.

The Revd Edward McAll, Rector of Brighstone 1846–1867.

Miss Catherine Moberly, daughter of George Moberly.

The Rt Revd. George Moberly, Rector of Brighstone 1867–1869, and then Bishop of Salisbury.

The Revd. Robert Leslie Morris, Rector of Brook and Mottistone, 1892–1909.

The Revd. John Pellow Gaze, Rector of Brook, 1856–1892.

General Jack Seely, The First Lord Mottistone. Died 1947.

The Revd. Ernest Silver, Rector of Brighstone 1903–1933.

The Rt Revd. Samuel Wilberforce, Rector of Brighstone 1830–1840, and later Bishop of Oxford, and then Winchester.

Mrs Paula Woodford, resident of Gaggerhill. Died 2002.

Printed sources

Books concerning the seasons of the Christian year are widely available. One of my favourites is *The Oxford Companion to the Year* (OUP 1999).

Local books concerning the villages of Brighstone, Brook and Mottistone are surprisingly numerous.

The *Brighstone Banner of Faith* first appeared in January, 1888, and became a victim of the First World War, making its final appearance in December 1916. Sadly, I can find no record of anything replacing it until the first *Brighstone News Sheet* of January 1962. This single page sheet has gradually expanded into its present format, extending to Brook and Mottistone in 1978, and to Shorwell in 1983. The Revd. Harvey Grindon is the only 20th century Rector of Brighstone for whom I cannot find any written records, and it is unfortunate that he cannot be included in *A Brighstone Book of Seasons*.

Writings by the Rectors of Brook and Mottistone have

been harder to find. Their contributions to the Banner of Faith are more in the form of official notices than items worthy of reproduction. I have managed to include a few items.

Other sources include

The Prose Works of Thomas Ken, edited by Rev. W. Benham

Parochial Sermons, mainly from Brighstone, by Bishop George Moberly

Dulce Domum (1911), by Catherine Moberly – a biography of her father.

A Life of Samuel Wilberforce (1883), by A.R. Ashwell

Fear and be Slain (1937), by General Jack Seely, 1st Lord Mottistone

Paths of Happiness (1938), by General Jack Seely, 1st Lord Mottistone

Brighstone in the Nineteenth Century (1983), by Dorothy Brooke

The Lifeboats of Brighstone Bay (1985), by Christopher Willis and Edward Roberts

Pot-Pourri of Poems (1992), by Richard J. Hutchings

Skipping like Rams (1994), by Elisabeth Heward Bowyer

Brooke Life Boat (1997), by Robert Cassell

Brighstone Village (2004), by Brighstone Village Museum Committee

All Play and No Work? A History of Brighstone's Schools (2004), by Dennis Courtney

Brighstone . . . and afterwards, by Rollo Lempriere